THE COMPLETE GUIDE TO
E-Security

For Joni.
Timeless beauty that nothing could improve.

THE COMPLETE GUIDE TO E-Security

PROTECT YOUR PRIVACY ON THE INTERNET

MICHAEL CHESBRO

CITADEL PRESS
Kensington Publishing Corp.
www.kensingtonbooks.com

Also by Michael E. Chesbro:
*Privacy for Sale: How Big Brother and Others Are
    Selling Your Private Secrets for Profit*

CITADEL PRESS books are published by

Kensington Publishing Corp.
850 Third Avenue
New York, NY 10022

Copyright © 2000 Michael E. Chesbro

All rights reserved. No part of this book may be reproduced in any form or by any means without the prior written consent of the publisher, excepting brief quotes used in reviews.

All Kensington titles, imprints, and distributed lines are available at special quantity discounts for bulk purchases for sales promotions, premiums, fund-raising, educational, or institutional use. Special book excerpts or customized printings can also be created to fit specific needs. For details, write or phone the office of the Kensington special sales manager: Kensington Publishing Corp., 850 Third Avenue, New York, NY 10022. attn: Special Sales Department, phone 1-800-221-2647.

Citadel Press and the Citadel logo are trademarks of Kensington Publishing Corp.

First Citadel printing: October 2001

10 9 8 7 6 5 4 3 2 1

Printed in the United States of America

Cataloging data for this title may be obtained from the Library of Congress.

ISBN 0-8065-2279-8

Table of Contents

Chapter 1: The Need for Private Communication 1
Chapter 2: Understanding E-Mail and the Internet 5
    Internet Protocol
    E-Mail Traps
    Trace Route
    Effective Use of Passwords
    Junk E-Mail, Pornography, and Spam
    Anonymous Web-Browsing
    Online People Finders
Chapter 3: Free E-Mail Services 29
    HushMail
    SAFe-mail
    ZipLip
    Unencrypted Web-Based E-Mail
    Juno
Chapter 4: Remailers 41
Chapter 5: Understanding Encryption 51
Chapter 6: PGP and Digital Certificates 57
Chapter 7: One-Time Pads 73
Chapter 8: Encryption Programs 85
    Norton Secret Stuff
    Security Box
    Two Fish Lite—with Key Generator
    Passwords and Encryption Built into Other Software
    Steganography
Chapter 9: Securely Deleting or Hiding Files 103
Chapter 10: Communications Planning 111

The Complete Guide to E-Security

Chapter 11: Online Communications and the Law
                Privacy in the E-World and the Physical World . .115
Chapter 12: A Final Word 123
Appendix I: FBI Statement on Encryption 127
Appendix II: Online Security and Privacy Resources 133
Appendix III: Title 18 United States Code,
                Sections 2701-2711 137
Appendix IV: 155
Bibliography 163

Foreword

Inevitable technological leaps continue to occur, dangerously blurring society's judgment as if intoxicated by sweet technology. The false senses of security that exist foster a blind reliance and unknowing addiction to e-commerce, e-mail, and e-recreation. A blatant disregard for security in the name of convenience is the result. This disregard is threatening our personal, industrial, and national security. If for one second we quantified the number of bits of sensitive information transiting the many Internet service providers worldwide, we would be astounded. The United States has an unhealthy infatuation and a severe security shortcoming with regard to the e-world. These security shortcomings will result in many of our fellow Americans paying a hefty price for unawareness. Loss of privacy, assets, and even, in extreme cases, life will occur if the potentially destructive technology threats are not understood and the vigilant countermeasures described in this book are not applied to our daily routines. This book will do wonders to overcome anyone's naiveté and offer a shocking grounding to simple techniques and practices that will exponentially increase personal security and safety in the Information Age.

Agent Myah Strong
Senior Intelligence Officer
U.S. Department of Defense

A Note About Internet Addresses

> "The principle that a man's home is his castle is under new attack. For centuries the law of trespass protected a man's lands and his home. But in this age of advanced technology, thick walls and locked doors cannot guard our privacy or safeguard our personal freedom."
> —Lyndon B. Johnson

In writing this book I have listed various Internet addresses, shareware programs, and sources of information. At the time I wrote about particular topics or listed Internet addresses or resources, the information was current and accurate. However, like postal mailing addresses and telephone numbers, these things may change with time. The fact that an address changes does not, however, mean the information itself has become useless. It is usually a simple matter of using a general search engine to find the new address of the information you are seeking (much like using a telephone directory to look up the new telephone number of a business).

There are many general search engines available on the Internet, any one of which may locate the information you are looking for. On the other hand, a single search engine may not find everything. If you do not find information you are searching for using one search engine, simply try another. But moving

The Complete Guide to E-Security

from one search engine to another and entering your search string each time can take a bit of time, as well as be a bit of an annoyance. The answer to this problem is simply to use a multi-search engine to submit your search string to several search engines at one time. The multi-search engine I have found most useful is Dogpile at http://www.dogpile.com. Dogpile submits your search to several major search engines and then displays the returned results.

Dogpile submits your search to the following search engines, and gives you the option of searching Web metasearch, Web catalog, Usenet, FTP, Newscrawler, BizNews, and more.

About.Com	**http://www.about.com**
Alta Vista	**http://www.altavista.com**
Direct Hit	**http://www.directhit.com**
Dogpile Web Catalog	**http://www.dogpile.com**
Dogpile Open Directory	**http://www.dogpile.com/opendir/index.html**
GoTo.Com	**http://www.goto.com**
Infoseek	**http://www.infoseek.go.com**
Looksmart	**http://www.looksmart.com**
Lycos	**http://www.lycos.com**

One other consideration with the information found in this book is *caveat emptor*, or, "let the buyer beware." This maxim states that you must view, judge, and test for yourself to determine the value and worth of any product or service.

By using the information provided here, you may significantly enhance your personal security and privacy, but it is important to remember that no system is perfect. Circumstances vary from place to place and from person to person, so I urge you to carefully examine all the information presented and practice before using these techniques in important or sensitive matters in your life.

Chapter 1

The Need for Private Communication

> *"The Government has been in bed with the entire telecommunications industry since the '40s. They've infected everything. They can get into your bank statements, computer files, e-mail, listen to your phone calls. Every wire, every airwave. The more technology you use, the easier it is for them to keep tabs on you. It's a brave new world out there—or at least it better be!"*
> —Gene Hackman as Brill in Enemy of the State

In 1791, when the founding fathers of the United States established our Constitution, communication took place between individuals either verbally or via the printed word. People could express any idea, discuss political topics, offer support or dissent to any belief, or conduct business, all with the understanding that privacy was a necessary and expected component of these conversations.

While the First Amendment to the Constitution guarantees our *right* to free speech, in order for free speech to take place and for speakers to be truly free in their expression, it is essential that individuals be allowed to take measures to ensure the privacy of their conversations. No individual, private enterprise, or government agency should be able to intercept, monitor, or record conversations you intend to be private and secure.

In 1791, two people could obtain a high degree of security in their personal communication simply by using a bit of common sense and paying attention to who might be around to overhear their conversation or intercept a written message. Today, however, while advances in technology have made communication much more efficient, ensuring the security of that communication now requires a specific and continued effort.

With the ever-growing popularity of the Internet and personal computers, e-mail has become an increasingly common form of communication. Most businesses and many homes have computers with access to e-mail and the Internet. Even if you don't have your own computer and work in a job that does not provide you with e-mail or Internet access, you can still create your own e-mail address using Web based e-mail and gain access through public libraries, cybercafés, or other public access systems. Because just about anyone who wants it can get some type of e-mail access, we need to understand how e-mail works and be aware of ways to secure these communications from unwanted intrusions.

Unwanted intrusions into your computer system and private communications can come from many sources. There are family members, friends, and coworkers with access to your computer system who mean no real harm but are, perhaps, a little too curious. There are criminals seeking to steal your passwords, credit card numbers, and other personal information for various nefarious purposes. On one major ISP you will be subject to almost weekly attempts to trick you into revealing your password, as well as a constant flood of pornographic e-mail. Complaints filed with the service provider do little good.

And, of course, there is the federal government, which goes to great efforts to ensure that American citizens can have few, if any, private communications. An article in the August 20, 1999, edition of *The Washington Post* shows just how far the government is willing to go to invade your right to privacy. The article by Robert O'Harrow Jr. is titled: "Justice Department Pushes for Power to Unlock PC Security Systems; Covert Acts Could Target Homes, Offices." The article details how the Justice Department

The Need for Private Communication

is seeking passage of laws that would let it conduct covert action against suspects' homes to disable security on their personal computers, thereby making it possible to secretly monitor their private communications over the Internet "as a prelude to a wiretap or further search." Personally, it makes me a little nervous to think that the same federal agencies that are responsible for the atrocity at Ruby Ridge, Idaho, where Vicki Weaver was shot in the face by an FBI sniper as she stood unarmed, cradling her nursing baby and the massacre of men, women, and children at the church in Waco, Texas, are now planning covert action against American citizens in their homes.

The FBI has long opposed private citizens having strong encryption, unless of course the FBI has a copy of the encryption key or some backdoor to defeat the security of the encryption program itself. Its argument runs something along the line of: "Terrorists, drug dealers, and other criminals use strong encryption, which prevents us from intercepting their communications, so we oppose making strong encryption available to any private citizen unless the government has a way to break that encryption." (A copy of a statement by the director of the FBI regarding the impact of encryption on law enforcement and public safety may be found in Appendix I of this book.)

Even if we accept the arguments of the FBI against private use of strong encryption, we still face potential intrusion into our private affairs when the encryption-breaking method law enforcement wants to use to fight crime falls into the hands of the criminals themselves.

Furthermore, we have to ask ourselves if we can trust the integrity of some of our government agencies. According to an April 1997 article in *Wired News*, 1,515 IRS employees were investigated in 1994 and 1995 for unauthorized snooping through taxpayer records. This was not a matter of one or two bad employees, but lawlessness so pervasive that the matter was addressed in the U.S. Senate! The General Accounting Office reported that the IRS continues to have serious weaknesses in

The Complete Guide to E-Security

safeguarding taxpayer data. If we can't trust the government to protect our Constitutional rights, if we can't trust the IRS not to snoop through our tax records, do we want to allow our public servants the ability to intrude on our private communications?

To counter intrusions into your private life and private communications it is important to understand just how these communications work. You must be aware of security programs and procedures that you can employ to increase the security of your private communications, and then you must implement these programs and procedures into your everyday communications. Let's begin by looking at the Internet and security of your e-mail communications.

Chapter 2

Understanding E-Mail and the Internet

> *"Any sound that Winston made, above the level of a very low whisper, would be picked up by it. . . . There was of course no way of knowing whether you were being watched at any given moment. . . . You had to live—did live, from habit that became instinct—in the assumption that every sound you made was overheard and, except in darkness, every movement scrutinized."*
>
> *—George Orwell, 1984*

Every computer connected to the Internet must have a unique address to distinguish it from other computers online and allow proper routing of information between these computers. This unique address is called an Internet protocol or simply an IP address.

INTERNET PROTOCOL

You can think of an IP address as being much like a telephone number. Each IP address consists of four number groups, with the numbers in each group ranging from 0 to 255. (For example, 140.47.5.4.) If you know the IP address of a site, but not the name, or if the site is not using a domain name, you can get to the site by simply typing in the IP address. For example, if you were to type **http://140.47.5.4** into your browser it would take you to the public Web page of the Defense Intelligence Agency. Of course, if you know its domain name you can also type **http://www.dia.mil.**

IP addresses may be divided into two types: static IP addresses and dynamic IP addresses. Those of us with a fixed connection to the Internet, such as private companies, or who use cable modems have static IP addresses. That is, our IP address stays the same no matter when we go online. Those of us using a dial-up service, such as America Online (AOL), Mindspring, Earthlink, and CompuServe, have dynamic IP addresses. When you dial into your AOL account, for example, you are assigned an IP address from a pool of addresses controlled by AOL. As long as you stay connected to the Internet you will use that particular IP address. When you log off, the IP address is returned to the pool controlled by AOL. The next time you connect to your account you are again assigned an IP address from those controlled by your ISP, but it probably won't be the same one you had before. (Your ISP very likely maintains a log of which of its IP addresses was assigned to whom and at what time. So dynamic IP addresses do not make you invisible to anyone putting forth enough effort to trace you.)

When you are "surfing the Internet" you are not typing in IP addresses. Rather you are typing in the names of the sites you want to visit, for example, **http://www.skye.com.** These names are called domain names and are an optional feature used to make the Internet a little more user-friendly. When you type in the name of your favorite Web site the name is converted to an IP address by a domain name server (DNS) that allows you to connect to the site. This is a semi-invisible process to the average user, although your Web browser may display the IP address as it is connecting. Domain names are tied directly to their IP addresses through the registration process, with the DNS being funded by registration fees for these names.

Domain names can be traced to their IP addresses by using a WHOIS database. There are various WHOIS databases available online. By running a WHOIS search against the domain name

```
           DICK'S SPORTING GOODS
               STERLING, VA
              (703) 433-2190


          101    006 41487   12/17/03
SALE                 7454    03:04 PM


FORMULA sz 3-8
  047791265423                  39.99
ASSOCIATE NUMBER #: 4867

    1 ITEMS    SUBTOTAL          39.99
  39.99  4.5%                     1.80
               TOTAL            $41.79
               VISA              41.79


   THANK YOU FOR SHOPPING AT DICK'S
   SHOP WWW.DicksSportingGoods.COM
```

Understanding E-Mail and the Internet

you will receive information about that domain. In this case if you ran a WHOIS search against the fictional domain name www.skye.com, you might see identifying information that looked like this:

Registrant:
Skye, Inc.
PO BOX 1234
Anytown, CO 80306

Domain Name: SKYE.COM

Administrative Contact:
Marie, Skye (SM0923) **skye@SKY.COM**
(303) 555-1212

Technical Contact, Zone Contact:
Network, Administrator (NET-ADMIN)
   netadmin@SKYE.NET
(303) 555-1100
Fax-(303) 555-9999

Record last updated on 23-Mar-1993.
Record created on 23-Mar-1993.
Database last updated on 29-Mar-2000 16:22:41 EST.

Domain servers in listed order:
NS1.SKYE.NET 166.98.1.9
NS2.SKYE.NET 166.98.8.6

As you can see from this WHOIS inquiry, you can obtain a fair amount of information about a domain from its registration information. Then it is a simple matter to contact the administrator of that domain to obtain additional information about activity on that system.

Some places to find WHOIS databases are

http://www.geektools.com/whois.html
http://www.betterwhois.com
http://swhois.net

You can find additional WHOIS databases by using a general search engine to search for the word "WHOIS."

E-MAIL TRAPS

E-mail traps take advantage of look-alike addresses to trick you into misdirecting your e-mail. For example, the (fictional) Acme Group may establish a domain of "acme.org" and create the e-mail address **info@acme.org** for general inquiries. Now, if I am interested in causing a little mischief with the Acme Group, I can create a domain of "acme.com" and set up an e-mail address of **info@acme.com**. Someone who wants to send e-mail to the Acme Group may believe that **info@acme.com** is, in fact, the correct address for the Acme Group, or may simply make the mistake of typing ".com" when he intended ".org." No matter, I am now receiving e-mail intended for the Acme Group. Taking this a step further, I may create a Web page at **http://www.acme.com**. This can trick more people into believing that I am the Acme Group. If the Acme Group has its real Web site at **http://www.acme.org** I can even copy their site to my Acme.com Web site to further confuse those wanting to deal with the real Acme Group. E-mail traps and faked Web sites are a common trick used by criminals online looking to steal your account log-in and password information, credit card numbers, and other personal information.

What about individuals, as opposed to companies? Pretending to be a specific individual is easier than pretending to be a group or business of some type. Let's take a look at Mr.

Understanding E-Mail and the Internet

John Doe, who has an e-mail address of **Jdoe@domain.com**. Wanting people to believe that I am Mr. Doe, I can create an e-mail address of **DoeJ@domain.com**, or perhaps **J_Doe@domain.com**. Someone receiving e-mail from one of these fake addresses may believe that it is actually from Mr. Doe and may reply to the fake address with requested information. (This is one important reason to encrypt all of your e-mail. While it is very simple to fake an e-mail address, it becomes much more difficult to fake properly managed encryption keys.)

> *"You have plenty of rights in this country, provided you don't get caught exercising them."*
> —Terry Mitchell, *The Revolutionary Toker*

TRACE ROUTE

When you send e-mail, it doesn't travel directly from your computer to the computer of whomever you have addressed your message to. It passes through many other computers along the pathway to its intended recipient. To view the pathway a message may take from your computer you can use the traceroute command under DOS.

While connected to the Internet, open the DOS window on your computer. You can do this by clicking on the MS-DOS prompt on your Programs Menu if you are using Windows 95/98/NT. In the DOS window type: tracert computer.name In this case "computer.name" will be the domain name of the e-mail recipient's computer (such as aol.com or mindspring.com). If you have not run a trace route before, you will likely be surprised at the number of computers through which your e-mail passes on the way to its recipient. Every one of these computers has access to the content of your message, and it seems likely that your message will become a permanent part of the archive and backup files of at least a few of them.

The Complete Guide to E-Security

Furthermore there is nothing to prevent the administrator of any of the systems through which your e-mail passes from reading it. Programs may be installed to search e-mail addresses, credit card numbers, key words, or specific text. Yes, there are laws which proscribe reading someone else's e-mail, but that doesn't mean it isn't happening.

Now, if the entire content of your e-mail message was "Happy Birthday Aunt Sally," you may not care that it has become part of an archive, accessible to some system administrator you have never even heard of before. On the other hand, if you were saying sweet nothings to your special someone, discussing your personal finances, planning a business deal, or any number of other private things, would you really want some stranger having access to your communications?

As an example, below is the route from an AOL account to a Mindspring account.

```
c:\ tracert mindspring.com
Tracing route to mindspring.com [207.69.200.66]
over a maximum of 30 hops:
  1  369 ms  359 ms  337 ms  ipt-fy8.proxy.aol.com
                             [205.188.200.105]
  2  379 ms  337 ms  358 ms  tot2-dr3.proxy.aol.com
                             [205.188.200.125]
  3  433 ms  360 ms  359 ms  tpopd-rri1.red.aol.com
                             [205.188.128.81]
  4  418 ms  338 ms  339 ms  pop1-dtc-P8-0.atdn.net
                             [204.148.99.221]
  5  456 ms  360 ms  360 ms  uunetgw1-P7-0.rre.aol.com
                             [205.188.130.70]
  6  337 ms  339 ms  358 ms  133.ATM2-
                             0.XR2.TCO1.ALTER.NET [146.188.161.198]
  7  395 ms  357 ms  359 ms  152.63.32.218
  8  356 ms  938 ms  378 ms  115.ATM7-
                             0.TR2.ATL1.ALTER.NET [146.188.138.189]
```

Understanding E-Mail and the Internet

9 434 ms 379 ms 378 ms 298.ATM7-
0.XR2.ATL1.ALTER.NET [146.188.232.109]
10 355 ms 399 ms 379 ms 194.ATM4-
0.GW6.ATL3.ALTER.NET [146.188.233.213]
11 456 ms 400 ms 379 ms cisco-1-p0-1-
0.atl2.mindspring.net [157.130.29.194]
12 355 ms 359 ms 378 ms mindspring.com
[207.69.200.66]
Trace complete.

As you can see, a message would travel through 12 different computers to make it from AOL to Mindspring. Once your message is on the Mindspring system it will likely pass through a few more computers within the Mindspring system itself before making it to the intended recipient.

You should think of e-mail as being like a postcard, copies of which are being made at the various post offices it passes through on the way to your mailbox. With this in mind, you can begin to employ various methods to keep the content of your e-mail private.

> *"How can we account for our present situation unless we believe that men high in this government are concerting to deliver us to disaster? This must be the product of a great conspiracy, a conspiracy on a scale so immense as to dwarf any previous such venture in the history of man. A conspiracy of infamy so black that, when it is finally exposed, its principals shall be forever deserving of the maledictions of all honest men."*
> —Congressional Record, 82nd Congress, page 6,602

EFFECTIVE USE OF PASSWORDS

One of the keys to online security is the effective use of passwords. Access to your system and online accounts is all based on entering an appropriate password. If your password is

The Complete Guide to E-Security

weak, or if it can be easily guessed, your online security and privacy can easily be compromised. Thus, it is important to understand what makes an effective password.

First, your password must be long enough so that it may not be guessed simply by trying all possible combinations of password construction. This is called a brute-force attack. As an example, if your password is made up of only lowercase letters and is three letters in length, there are 17,576 possible passwords (26 x 26 x 26). If you were to increase the length of your password to merely four letters in length you get 456,976 possible passwords, and if you were to use a password of eight characters in length (which is the minimum length I recommend) you get 208,827,065,476 possible passwords. Of course you can make your password even more secure by including uppercase letters, numbers, and metacharacters (%, *, @, $, etc.). If you were to create a password that was eight characters in length compiled choosing from all 95 printable characters on the standard keyboard, you would have 6,634,204,312,890,625 possible password combinations. This many possible combinations effectively defeats any possibility of using a brute-force attack to determine your password.

Assuming you had a computer that could try a brute force attack against your password at 10,000 possibilities per second the following chart shows the maximum time it would take to break various password structures.

Password Length	Lowercase Only (a-z)	95 Characters (a-z, A-Z, 0-9 and metacharacters)	256 Characters All ASCII Characters
3	2 seconds	1 minute	27 minutes
4	1 minute	2.3 hours	4 days
5	19 minutes	9 days	3 years
6	8.6 hours	2 years	890 years
7	9 days	238 years	228,300 years
8	240 days	22,800 years	58,454,600 years
9	17 years	219,450 years	14,964,398,900 years
10	447 years	210,674,400 years	3,830,889,121,100 years

Understanding E-Mail and the Internet

Statistically, it should take only half the time listed to break the passwords using our computer processing 10,000 passwords per second, since it is unlikely that the computer will have to process every single possibility to find the correct answer. It should also be noted that most any modern computer could process 10,000 possibilities per second. Therefore, use long passwords!

There are certain things that make a password secure. A password should be at least eight characters in length. Using a passphrase—a short sentence—as you can with PGP is even better. PGP (Pretty Good Privacy) is a powerful encryption tool that will be explained in detail in following chapters.

A password must not be just a single word contained in a dictionary, no matter how long or uncommon that word is. Using a dictionary attack, it is possible to determine someone's password simply by trying every word in the dictionary. Since most people have a working vocabulary of only several thousand words and will pick a word with which they are familiar, a dictionary-based attack against a password will usually recover it in a matter of seconds. My dictionary contains about 96,000 words. Using our computer trying 10,000 possible words per second, someone could break a single-word password in about the time it takes to read this page. Even assuming that we increase our word list 10 times to account for variations on words and case sensitivity, we have only 960,000 possibilities to try. As you can see, it takes only a few minutes at most to break single-word, dictionary-based passwords. Because of the very short time it takes to run a dictionary attack against passwords, most people will try a dictionary attack first. So *never use a single word for your password!*

A password should contain at least one lowercase letter, one uppercase letter, one number, and one metacharacter. Once you have chosen your password you must *never* write it down! Memorize your password. If you simply can't remember it without writing it down, protect its written form with all possible security. Remember, however, that by writing down your password you degrade the effectiveness of your security by at least 60 percent! Written passwords may be discovered, lost, or obtained during a raid on your home or office (either with or without a warrant)!

An effective way to make an easily remembered password is to choose two words, separate them with a metacharacter, and precede or follow this with a number. For example: Privacy&Freedom:1776.

To enhance your password security, you should change your password whenever there is any possibility of compromise, and on a frequent but irregular basis as an added security precaution. I recommend that you change your password whenever you have logged into an account from a public terminal, or when there have been people standing nearby when you entered your password from a private terminal. You should also change your passwords at least every 30 to 90 days as a matter of course.

> *"It is the common fate of the indolent to see their rights made a prey by the active. The condition upon which God has given liberty to man is ETERNAL VIGILANCE: which condition if he breaks, servitude is at once the consequence of his crime, and the punishment of his guilt."*
>
> –J.P. Curran, 1790

JUNK E-MAIL, PORNOGRAPHY, AND SPAM

Sooner or later, if you use the Internet regularly, your e-mail address will be picked up by online advertisers, pornographers, and others who will begin to flood your mailbox with offers, solicitations, and just plain annoying e-mail messages.

Like postal junk mail, most unsolicited e-mail is of little or no interest to you, but instead of cluttering up a landfill, you can simply click "delete" without ever bothering to open it. Unfortunately, there comes a point when your online mailbox becomes flooded

Understanding E-Mail and the Internet

with unsolicited e-mail, requiring you to sort through the various subject lines and sender addresses in an attempt to cull the e-mail that you want to receive from the junk.

In addition to various businesses and groups sending you offers for their products or soliciting donations for their causes, we are faced with pornographers who use the Internet and e-mail to distribute their wares and solicit others to participate in their pornographic ventures.

Now, I strongly believe in the right of free speech, and I believe that people should be allowed to create Web sites to express any point of view. I believe that individuals should be able to discuss any topic using e-mail and other online communication without interference from government or threat of censorship. However, your right to free speech does not override my right to privacy—my right to be left alone. The right of an individual to maintain a pornographic Web site or send pornographic material to those who have requested it does not extend to distributing pornographic material to those who find it offensive, to children, or to using e-mail and the Internet to solicit children for sexual purposes.

It is clearly the intent of some online pornographers, and other junk e-mailers, to send material to individuals who do not wish to receive it. First, this material is sent out indiscriminately to e-mail addresses captured online from Web sites, chat rooms, and the like. Furthermore, these messages often have false and misleading subject lines. An e-mail message with the subject line "Hi . . . I just got online and wanted to let you know" may contain explicit and vulgar descriptions of a pornographic site, with embedded links to that site. Is it likely that you will open this message to see if some friend or colleague has just got online? Do your children have their own e-mail addresses? How likely is it that children may open this type of innocent sounding message? Often pornographic e-mail is specifically targeted at children and contains false and misleading subject lines in order to entice them into sexual situations.

The Complete Guide to E-Security

Online pornographers are not the only ones to use false and misleading headers and subject lines to get you to read their e-mail or click on links to their sites. This type of thing is becoming more common even among what were once considered to be reputable businesses.

The law is quite clear regarding the use of the postal service to distribute offensive or unwanted material. However, when it comes to e-mail we enter a gray area with little established case law or regulation. In most cases, you are on your own. There are, however, some things that you can do to fight junk e-mail, pornographers, and spam online, thereby helping ensure your online privacy.

- First, use the various techniques described throughout this book. PGP encryption, anonymous servers, and remailers all serve to make you less visible online. Obviously, if your e-mail address cannot be determined, no one can send you unsolicited e-mail.

- If you receive unsolicited or offensive e-mail, forward the e-mail to the postmaster of the domain from which the material was sent. Most ISPs have established policies against sending unsolicited or offensive e-mail and will take action against the offending account if they receive enough complaints. The domain is simply the last part of the e-mail address. If you received unsolicited e-mail from **spammer@spam.com**, you should forward the offending e-mail to **postmaster@spam.com**. You may also wish to register complaints with various government agencies asking that they take action against the offending domain.

You may wish to adapt the following sample letter for your own use when registering complaints about offensive e-mail:

Understanding E-Mail and the Internet

Postmaster@spam.com

It is our understanding that Spam.Com is a corporation organized and existing under the laws of the State of Delaware with its principal place of business at 123 Spam Blvd., Dulles, Virginia 20160. Spam.Com sends, or permits its services to be used to send, pornographic material to children. Although we have reported this criminal activity to Spam.Com, Spam.Com continues to send, or continues to allow its services to be used to send unsolicited pornographic material to Spam.Com customers. Based on Spam.Com's failure to stop sending pornographic material, or to prevent its services from being used to send pornographic material to its customers, we are forwarding copies of all unsolicited pornographic material received to the Attorney General of the State Delaware & Virginia, Federal Trade Commission, Federal Bureau of Investigation, and to other government agencies and elected officials, requesting they take such action as may be necessary to protect our children from sexual predators using Spam.Com Services.

The extreme amount of unsolicited pornographic material sent from Spam.Com accounts is highly offensive, and of a nature to threaten the public order. Criminal laws prohibit the sale or distribution over computer networks of obscene material (18 U.S.C. 1465, 1466, 2252 and 2423(a)). By failing to take positive and direct action against those using Spam.Com services for criminal purposes, we believe that Spam.Com may be held liable under the law for this criminal conduct. We further believe that Spam.Com is in violation of the Computer Fraud & Abuse Act (18 U.S.C. 1030 et.esq.), the Virginia Computer Crimes Act (VA Code Ann. Section 18.2-152.2 et.esq), and the Washington Commercial Electronic Mail Act (Wash. Rev. Code, Chapter 19.190 et. esq.)

Of even greater concern is the fact that this porno-

> graphic material is often directed specifically at children, or is sent to sites to which children have regular access. The law already proscribes the solicitation of minors over computers for any sexual activity (18 U.S.C. 2452) and illegal luring of minors into sexual activity through computer conversations (18 U.S.C. 2423(b)).
>
> We believe that Spam.Com has a duty to prevent its services from being used for criminal purposes. Each piece of unsolicited pornographic e-mail sent from a Spam.Com account violates federal and state law as cited above. Pornographic material sent for the purpose of the solicitation of minors, or the luring of minors into sexual activity not only violates the law cited above but is so shocking that no man not under delusion could accept this activity, allow it to continue, or remotely believe that such conduct did not grossly offend the public senses and the safety of the community.
>
> Because recipients of unsolicited pornographic electronic mail are unable to avoid the receipt of such mail through reasonable means, such mail clearly threatens the privacy and safety of recipients. This threat is enhanced for recipients whose electronic mail software or server alerts them to new mail as it arrives, since unsolicited pornographic electronic mail thereby disrupts the normal operation of the recipient's computer.
>
> Therefore we request that Spam.Com, and others in receipt of this notice, take immediate, clear, and positive steps to prevent the sexual stalking of our children through the use of Spam.Com services.

Now, it is clear that Spam.Com and 123 Spam Blvd. in Dulles, Virginia, is a fictional domain and street address for this ISP, but by using a WHOIS server to determine the address of an offending domain and replacing Spam.Com with the identification of the offending domain, you have an effective complaint form to battle unsolicited and offensive e-mail.

Understanding E-Mail and the Internet

- If your online software will allow it, block all e-mail to your account except from specifically designated addresses. Thus, any e-mail you receive at your personal e-mail address will be from an account that you have designated as one from which you want to receive correspondence.

- Establish an online business e-mail address where notifications and product advertisements can be sent. Expect to receive a lot of junk e-mail at this address.

On April 21, 2000 The Children's Online Privacy Protection Act (COPPA) became law, as codified in 15.U.S.C. Sec. 6501, et seq. COPPA spells out specific rules to protect the online privacy of children under the age of 13. It applies to Web site operators whose sites are specifically directed at children, and to sites of a general nature that children may access.

Specifically, the COPPA restricts individually identifiable information about a child that may be collected online, and if collected defines how that information may be used. This information includes such things as full name, home address, e-mail address, telephone number or any other information that would allow someone to identify or contact the child. The COPPA also applies to other information—for example, hobbies, interests and information collected through cookies or other types of tracking mechanisms—when that information is tied to individually identifiable information about the child. It requires verified parental consent to collect information from a child and provides that parents have the right to review said information as well as control its use or have it removed from databases.

Overall, I believe that the COPPA is a good law, with the intent of protecting our children online. If online marketers acted responsibly such a law would not be necessary, but since they often lack any degree of reasonableness in their marketing or even specifically target children, COPPA is a step in the right direction (for the full text of the COPPA, see Appendix IV at the back of this book).

Some may ask whether it is worth the effort to file complaints against online pornographers and spammers. I believe it is essential to e-security that we take action to prevent unsolicited e-mail from flooding the Information Superhighway. There will always be individuals and businesses who seek to invade your personal privacy, but by taking action against these criminals we help enhance security online. If ISPs receive a sufficient number of complaints about their lack of security policies they may be forced to develop effective programs to protect their customers. Furthermore, by making various government agencies aware of ISPs who allow their systems to be used for criminal purposes, we assist in the development of laws to protect ourselves from online criminals.

Personally, I believe that the Internet can be, and in fact should be, self-governing without excessive government regulation. The problem, however, is that the major ISPs do little, if anything, to prevent their systems from being used for criminal purposes, and perhaps even less to protect the privacy of those individuals who subscribe to their services.

> "The information highway is also invading our homes, tapping into our personal lives. . . . They can and do build dossiers and secret files on us that threaten our most cherished freedoms."
> –Grant R. Jeffrey, *Final Warning*

THOSE DAMN POP-UP ADS . . . HIDDEN DANGERS!

We have all seen them: windows that open on our browser as we try to look at some page on the Internet. We didn't ask to look at the content of the new window. It probably has nothing to do with what we were originally trying to look at. It's just some advertiser hawking this product or that site, and keeping us from doing what we logged into the Internet to do in the first place. You've just been victimized by an Internet "pop-up ad!"

Understanding E-Mail and the Internet

Okay . . . we all pretty much agree that pop-up ads are annoying, but are there any risks associated with running this type of advertising on our computers? Unfortunately, the answer is *yes*. A pop-up is a script (read program) running on your computer that you did not choose to run. This is in and of itself enough reason to be concerned, but there are even greater reasons to be concerned. Many pop-up ads do more than just open a window to advertise this or that. They introduce a malicious script into your computer causing it to do things that you don't want it to do. The techniques, begun by Internet porn sites, include throwing you into an endless loop of pop-up ads, hijacking your browser's default homepage, downloading unwanted software to your system, and working to capture your e-mail address (thereby allowing you to be flooded with unsolicited commercial e-mail or SPAM). These deplorable techniques are no longer used just by porn sites, but now by sites that one might have once thought were respectable businesses.

But wait . . . the worst is yet to come. Not satisfied with annoying you on a given page, to which you might choose not to return because of its pop-ups, the wizards of Internet advertising have come up with a new technique to take over your computer. Now when you visit a site, you may find that it has run a small JavaScript causing pop-up ads to begin appearing on your computer several minutes later, even after you have left the site that started the script. This can cause you to believe pop-up ads are being run from a site that has nothing to do with them.

The way this little time bomb works is to open a small window, say 1x1, at some location that will not normally be visible on your computer screen, say at 10,000 x 10,000, following the "on-upload" command when you visit a site. Now you use the "back" button on your browser, or type in a new URL moving to a new site. Off screen and continuing its countdown is our JavaScript time bomb. All of a sudden a pop-up ad appears from a site where you would never expect such trash. Closing this pop-up can cause another to open, all the while using up your valu-

The Complete Guide to E-Security

able time and your computer resources to support their advertising.

According to an article by Leslie Walker, "Pop-Up Ads Downright Annoying," in the April 5, 2001 edition of the *Washington Post,* one of the companies behind these advertising time bombs is Internet Fuel of Los Angeles and its affiliate marketing program "ExitFuel." According to Walker, even if you like the product being advertised you may not get what you ask for. One of the ads offered to download a "browser enhancement" and showed a media player. Unfortunately what you get by downloading this browser enhancement is a program designed to show even more ads!

Pop-up ads and hidden JavaScript to run them are the same as Trojans and denial of service attacks. Remember, a Trojan is a program that purports to do one thing while actually doing something else, or including some additional unwanted function. A denial of service attack is an attack that keeps you from efficiently using your computer resources. If you are trying to use your computer and pop-up ads get in the way, those ads deny you use of your computer until you close them, or move them out of the way. Pop-up ads can also cause your browser to crash if a significant number of them open concurrently. (Crashing your browser is actually fairly common with pop-ups.) If you pay for your online time by the hour, any time spent dealing with pop-up ads is directly costing you money. This loss of money is significant enough that Judge Frederika Smith of the Miami-Dade County Court allowed a class action suit to proceed against America Online (AOL) because AOL pop-up ads prevented AOL customers from effectively using their computer time.

As we have seen, Internet pop-up ads are much more than a minor nuisance, but what can we do about them? First, set your browser security protocols to high, and be sure JavaScripting is disabled. This will solve some of the problem, but may limit legitimate functions on some sites. In this case you may want to add these sites to a "trusted sites list" allowing JavaScript to run from

Understanding E-Mail and the Internet

these sites only. I run high security across the board when online, and don't personally find it to be a problem, but you may find that your Internet preferences are different.

You should also download software to combat these malicious pop-up programs. There are several programs available, all of which do pretty much the same thing. A couple of programs that I like, offering both freeware and commercial versions are Adsubtract (**www.adsubtract.com**) and Webwasher (**www.webwasher.com**).

Finally, don't deal with any company that wastes your time and money with pop-up ads. These companies probably aren't the most reputable anyway since they hijack your computer to hawk their sites and products.

ANONYMOUS WEB-BROWSING

Whenever you visit a Web site on the Internet you expose yourself to an invasion of your personal privacy. Information that may be collected about you when you visit a Web site includes, but is not limited to, your IP address, geographical location, e-mail address, viewing habits on that site, other sites visited, type of computer equipment you are using, and ISP. This information can be collected in various ways, but let's take a look at something common to many Web sites: the cookie.

Most Internet users have seen the term "cookie." Simply put, a cookie is a little ID tag placed on your computer when you visit various Web sites. Now, in and of itself a cookie is not particularly dangerous. It is a small text file (usually around 100 bytes) that a Web site may send to your computer that tells them whether you have visited before whenever you log on to their site. It identifies what preferences you may have set last time, and can save information such as selections you added to a "shopping cart" on an online store site. The purpose of cookies is to prevent you from having to log on and/or set preferences every time you return to a particular Web site. Because it is just a small text file, a cookie cannot transmit a virus to your computer. Cookies are also not supposed to be able to be read by any site other than the one that places it there, but there have been bugs that allowed sites to view cookies that were created by others. Over a period of time you will get a considerable number of cookies on your system. If you want to see what cookies you have they are normally stored in a folder called "Cookies" under your "Windows" directory.

Here is an example of what a cookie looks like:

ksa
0OUG5-9FVA5kAAKSNRBs02841099
valueclick.com/
0
870820224
31184131
1513647776
29348494
*

One of the best examples of the use of cookies and tracking on a Web site is Amazon.Com. When you log on to the Amazon Web site a cookie is sent to your computer. In order to make purchases you must, of course, register. Once you have done so, Amazon will greet you by name when you next visit its site. As you make purchases from Amazon it develops a profile about you based on your purchases, and thereafter will make recommendations of other products that may be of interest to you. The more you shop with Amazon the better its profile of you becomes. Its recommendations usually match your interests quite well.

However, the next time someone visits the Amazon site from a computer containing my Amazon cookie, the site thinks that *I* am making this connection and greets me by name. It also makes recommendations for me in books, music, and more. Now, to be fair, it takes a password before anyone can place an online order,

Understanding E-Mail and the Internet

but do you really want just anyone to be able to browse through your preferences in "books, music, and more . . ."?

But sites like Amazon pose only a very minor concern when compared to the potential invasion of your privacy by such major Internet advertisers as "DoubleClick." (If you have more than a few cookies on your computer it is very likely that one is from DoubleClick.) The cookie contains no personal identifying information, but does serve as an identifying tag that allows DoubleClick to track that cookie (and thus the computer/user where the cookie is located) across the 1,500 or so sites in the DoubleClick network. Sites in the DoubleClick Network include such sites as AltaVista, Travelocity, and the Multex Investment Network.

Now, some readers may be thinking, "So what? Didn't you just say that the cookie contains no personal identifying information?" Yes, that's what I said, but don't call me paranoid just yet. In November 1999, DoubleClick merged with the direct marketing company Abacus Direct. Following the merger there were plans to join the Abacus Direct marketing database of names, addresses and other online shopper information with the DoubleClick database of anonymous Internet user profiles. As the old saying goes, "Houston, we have a problem!" Matching an anonymous Internet profile with marketing information obtained when you purchased something online or registered with a specific Web site means the cookies on your system are now linked directly to your personal identifying information!

I, along with many other privacy advocates, strongly protested the merging of these databases. The states of Michigan, New York, and Vermont have threatened to take legal action against DoubleClick if its information gathering practices are not changed, and the Federal Trade Commission (FTC) looked into the matter. Based on this public outcry, Kevin Ryan, the president of DoubleClick, said his company would postpone linking personally identifiable information to anonymous Internet profiles "until there is agreement between government and industry on privacy standards." Note, this does not mean that these databases will not end up being merged, simply that DoubleClick and the government need to look at what will become a standard for tracking you online.

Because of the ever-growing potential for businesses and government agencies to track you online, I recommend that you take steps to protect yourself from such invasions of privacy. One of the steps you can take is using the services of Anonymizer (**http://www.anonymizer.com**). Anonymizer gives you the ability to surf the Internet invisibly—Web sites you visit will simply have no way to automatically collect information about you. Anonymizer has been providing privacy and security services to the Internet community since 1996, and although it offers several services, it is known best for its anonymous Web-browsing service.

To use Anonymizer, simply go to its Web page and enter the address of the site you wish to visit anonymously. If you are a paid subscriber you will be asked to enter your user name and password and you'll be taken immediately to the site you've chosen. If you're surfing for free, you will be delayed several seconds but will soon be taken anonymously to the site requested. As long as you are accessing Web sites through Anonymizer you are invisible to those sites.

Anonymizer is well worth the small fee, and I recommend that anyone who regularly surfs the Internet sign up and take advantage of this fine service.

> "Freedom can exist only in the society of knowledge. Without learning, men are incapable of knowing their rights . . ."
> —Dr. Benjamin Rush, 1786

ONLINE PEOPLE FINDERS

There are several database/search engines available on the Internet that allow you to search for the address, telephone number, and e-mail address of any person. These services are called

Understanding E-Mail and the Internet

"people finders" and offer these basic searches for free. People-finder databases develop their information from telephone directories, public records, and information provided by people who use these services, making them useful for finding old friends, lost loves, or your old army buddy.

Each of the people-finder databases obtains information from its own sources, so it pays to check the databases you come across to find out if you are listed therein. All the databases will likely have a listing for anyone listed in the white pages of a telephone directory, but because they obtain information from other sources, you can often find unlisted telephone numbers. Most of the people-finder databases allow you to add yourself to the database, update information, and provide additional details (such as schools attended or hobbies).

Some people-finder databases can be found at the following Web sites:

http://www.555-1212.com
http://www.anywho.com
http://www.lookupusa.com
http://www.switchboard.com
http://www.whowhere.com
http://www.people.yahoo.com

This wealth of readily available personal information can, however, be a bane to people trying to live private lives. One possible option for the privacy seeker is to provide limited or false information to these databases. This may serve as a means of misdirecting anyone trying to locate you. Generally, however, I believe it is best not to appear in the databases at all—let there simply be no clue to follow for anyone trying to track you down.

The good news about these databases is that they are usually well run and will allow those who do not wish to be listed to have their information deleted.

Chapter 3

Free E-Mail Services

> *"Those who would give up essential liberty to purchase safety deserve neither liberty nor safety."*
> —Benjamin Franklin, 1759

There are two kinds of e-mail service available to you: Web-based and non-Web-based.

When you sign up with an online service (such as AOL, CompuServe, or Earthlink) you are provided with software to install on your computer and access to the networks run by these companies. This gives you access to the Internet, one or more e-mail addresses, and perhaps other services. This is a non-Web-based e-mail account. When you establish a Web-based e-mail account (such as Hotmail, Yahoo! Mail, HushMail, or ZipLip) you are provided with no software and usually pay no fees for the basic service but must provide your own access to the Internet and usually won't have the extra services of the non-Web-based ISPs.

The advantage to Web-based services is that you can access your e-mail from anywhere you can get access to the Internet. The services are generally free and offer you some degree of

The Complete Guide to E-Security

anonymity not found with a service with a monthly fee charged to your credit card or withdrawn from your bank account. But many of the traditionally non-Web-based services now allow you to access their e-mail through the Internet. As an example, if you are an AOL customer you can access your e-mail either from the AOL software you installed on your computer when you established your account or through the AOL Web site at **http://www.aol.com**.

Secure Socket Layer

Secure socket layer, or SSL, is a protocol originally developed by Netscape. Although there are other similar protocols, SSL has been universally accepted as the standard for encrypted communication and authentication between clients and servers. SSL actually contains two subprotocols, the record protocol and the handshake protocol. The record protocol defines the format in which data will be transmitted between the client and the server. The handshake is a series of messages sent between the client and server when they first establish their connection. Briefly, after the record protocol determines the transmission format, the handshake authenticates the server to the client. The client and server then determine which cryptographic algorithms are supported by both the client and the server. They will normally select the strongest algorithm that is mutually supported. The handshake then uses public key technology to develop a shared session key (shared secrets). These shared secrets are then used to establish the symmetric encryption key (master secret) and establish the encrypted SSL connection. The current algorithms (ciphers) used in SSL are

    Triple DES (168-bit encryption) with SHA-1
        message authentication
    RC-4 (128-bit encryption) with MD5 message authentication
    RC-2 (128-bit encryption) with MD5 message authentication
    IDEA (128-bit encryption) with MD5 message authentication

Free E-Mail Services

> DES (56-bit encryption) with SHA-1 message authentication
> RC-4 (40-bit encryption) with MD5 message authentication
> RC-2 (40-bit encryption) with MD5 message authentication
> No Encryption, with MD5 message authentication only
>
> The weaker (40-bit) RC-4 and RC-2 ciphers are to allow for export of the encryption technology, as US law prohibits export of stronger than 40-bit encryption. Triple-DES (using 3 passes of the DES cipher to encrypt) is by far the strongest cipher, but it is not as fast as RC-4, which tends to be the most commonly used cipher.
> The encryption function, once the SSL connection has been established, is invisible to the user. SSL runs on top of the TCP/IP layer but below the application protocols (such as HTTP, IMAP, or LDAP), so the user never sees the encrypted traffic.

HUSHMAIL

HushMail (**http://www.hushmail.com**) is a free, Web-based e-mail service that uses 1,024-bit encryption to secure communication between two HushMail accounts. It uses public key encryption but stores both the public and private keys on its own servers, which allows you to use HushMail from any computer, not just the one containing your private key. It also automatically encrypts messages between HushMail accounts, which means you don't have to remember to activate a security protocol or take any extra steps to protect your messages.

When you send e-mail from one HushMail account to another, your message is encrypted with the public key of the HushMail addressee before it is transmitted. This is accomplished through the Java applet you download to your computer when you access your HushMail account. Your messages are encrypted within the Java applet before being transmitted to the HushMail server. Encryption is based on the Blowfish algorithm, a 128-bit symmetric block cipher system. Because encryption is accomplished on your computer, not even HushMail employees will be able to read your messages. As long as the e-mail is being sent between HushMail accounts, the only things that should ever be on their servers are encrypted messages.

When the addressee opens his HushMail account to read your message, HushMail uses his private key and passphrase to decrypt the message. (HushMail will allow you to send e-mail to non-HushMail accounts but will not encrypt these messages because there is no public key associated with those addresses.)

Below is an example of a HushMail message as it is transmitted across the Internet before being decrypted at the recipient's account.

----- HushMail v1.11 -----
a50799774d781b2bcb3f65de8e7f1e50304d5b64df4acace7
23fb9b2cd6610150f3d5d7c7090a79bf7cf35e48cc0bf3ab6ba70
7eb004f4f2de436b19feb2c8a8f5451bf24b7d645049058b8d4d
12bf063dbb5d7d9db6c762dc9187827c731e1834c3f8089f6701
----- End -----

IMPORTANT NOTICE: If you are not using HushMail, this message could have been read easily by the many people who have access to your open personal email messages.

Get your FREE, totally secure email address at http://www.hushmail.com.

The use of a Java applet to encrypt your e-mail messages means that you must have a fairly up-to-date system. HushMail lists its system requirements as

Netscape Communicator 4.04 or better

Free E-Mail Services

Microsoft Internet Explorer 4.0 or better
AOL 5.0
Windows95, Windows98, or WindowsNT
Many Unix variants, such as Linux Kernel versions 2.0.x or 2.2.x

Another major advantage of using HushMail is that it shields your IP address from the recipient of the message. Someone receiving HushMail from you cannot determine its originating IP address. Since HushMail does not track the IP addresses of account holders and maintains no log of the IP addresses of anyone logging into the HushMail site, you have a shield against anyone tracking you through your HushMail account.

Also of great importance to the security of HushMail is the February 2001 announcement that Phil Zimmermann, the developer of PGP, has joined the HushMail team. Zimmermann's expertise in online security and his demonstrated commitment to individual freedom through private encryption makes HushMail even more appealing.

If you don't have a HushMail account, get one today. It's free, it's easy, and it keeps snoops out of your private e-mail by using cutting-edge technology!

SAFE-MAIL

Another online source for establishing a secure Web-based e-mail account is SAFe-mail (**http://www.safe-mail.net**). Developed by Galiad Computers, Ltd., and based in Jerusalem, Israel, SAFe-mail offers secure online communications integrated into a comprehensive online security package.

SAFe-mail uses a proprietary encryption scheme to protect information stored on its servers and SSL to secure all transmissions. Because SAFe-mail uses a proprietary encryption scheme, the strength of this encryption cannot be known. It must also be assumed that SAFe-mail employees have the capability to discov-

The Complete Guide to E-Security

er the content of all messages that pass through their servers. This is not really any different than any other Web-based e-mail system, in which the system administrator has the ability to read any plaintext (unecrypted text) message that passes through his system. (Unfortunately, this is also true for any outsider who can hack into the system and gain system administrator privileges.) SAFe-mail solves the problems of outside monitoring of communications on their system by using SSL for transmission and maintaining all stored messages in an encrypted format.

In addition to encrypted e-mail, SAFe-mail offers other features that make it very appealing to those seeking online security and privacy. SAFe-mail . . .

- does not require you to provide any identifying information when establishing an account. Simply choose a user name and make up a password. SAFe-mail provides the option of providing detailed information in a user profile for those individuals who want to have an e-mail account clearly identified as belonging to a specific person, but this information is not required to establish an account. However, it should be noted that header information in SAFe-mail messages contains your IP address, so messages are not anonymous!

- allows one user to "authenticate" another, thus establishing bona fides for that person. This has a similar function to the key-signing feature found in PGP. One other advantage of this authentication feature is that you may establish a closed group for communication, where all members of the group must be authenticated by a specific individual. Using this feature can ensure that all mail sent and received stays within the authenticated group.

- gives users an option of creating a bulletin board where SAFe-mail users can post and read messages. The creator of the bulletin board can restrict access to the bulletin board to

Free E-Mail Services

selected SAFe-mail users, thereby creating a private bulletin board for groups or organizations.

- has a message-tracking feature whereby a unique identification number is assigned to each message. This number is visible to all recipients of the message, thus allowing a specific message to be tracked and referenced. SAFe-mail further offers a message receipt/acknowledgment feature that notifies the sender of the message when it is opened by the recipient(s).

- offers an online chat function allowing real-time conferencing and conversations. Because SAFe-mail uses SSL for all data transmissions, outsiders cannot intercept or monitor these conversations.

- is based in Israel and governed under the laws of the State of Israel. This means anyone who wants to obtain information about your e-mail communications has to deal with the Israeli government.

I like SAFe-mail and believe that it offers a lot in the way of e-security. The infrastructure of the system seems to be well thought-out and well established. My only concern with SAFe-mail is its use of a proprietary encryption scheme as opposed to an established and tested system. This problem is very easily corrected for those concerned with personal online security—just use PGP to encrypt all of your messages before sending them through the SAFe-mail system. By using PGP within the SAFe-mail system you can take full advantage of SAFe-mail's security infrastructure while at the same time adding PGP's high-level encryption. This prevents even SAFe-mail's system administrator from being able to access the content of your communication. Remember, however, that this does not prevent other types of attack against your communications, such as traffic analysis or denial of service, and Israel is not an ally of the United States when it comes to matters of industry, science, and technology.

> "Because of what appears to be a lawful command on the surface, many citizens, because of their respect for the law, are cunningly coerced into waiving their rights, due to ignorance."
> —*U.S. v. Minker* 350 U.S. 179, 187

ZIPLIP

ZipLip (**http://www.ziplip.com**) bills itself as a secure and confidential snoop-proof e-mail system that combines the advantages of a Web-based e-mail server with the strong encryption of 128-bit SSL and the Blowfish or Triple-DES algorithms. An account comes with a wide variety of services and options.

When you use ZipLip's security features, you are provided with a program called STEP: Shredding, Tracking, Encryption, and Policy (or message management). With the security features turned off, it functions as a standard Web-based e-mail server like Hotmail or Yahoo! mail.

When you log into your account, ZipLip secures your time online using SSL. You prepare your message by typing it into the text block. (You can also paste text from your clipboard. Think PGP encrypted text here . . . hint, hint!) You also have the option of attaching files to your message.

ZipLip stores your message in an encrypted format on the ZipLip server while waiting for it to be retrieved.

When you send your message using ZipLip's security features, ZipLip creates a mailbox on its server and stores your message there. ZipLip then alerts the addressee that he has a message and gives him the link to retrieve it.

You@your-address.com,
You have received a secure, private message at ZipLip.com.

Free E-Mail Services

Please click or copy-paste the following link into your browser to access the message.

http://www.ziplip.com/ps/PmApp/zlc_rf?messageId=oly1458 419811959238322976&ur=&usr=u13983670511

Sender: "E-Security" <esecurity@ziplip.com>
Subject: E-Security
Date Sent: Wednesday, May 24, 2000, 11:00 PM

If you have questions please send them to help@ziplip.com
http://www.ziplip.com/

To read the message, the addressee simply clicks on the link or copies it and pastes it into his browser. The message is then displayed (much like Web-based greeting cards).

You have the option of protecting your message with a password, which the recipient must enter in order to open the message. ZipLip allows a "password hint" line to be included with the message, but this also gives a clue to anyone else who may access the message. I recommend against using the password hint field to give a hint to the password, but it can be used to provide other brief information to the recipient before he opens the message.

ZipLip also provides a message expiration feature. This allows you to set a time after which your message will expire and be deleted from the ZipLip server. Current options for this function are

Message Does Not Expire
Message Expires in 1 day
Message Expires in 3 days
Message Expires in 1 week

Message Expires in 2 weeks
Message Expires in 30 days

This is an excellent security feature and ensures that someone cannot snoop into old messages that aren't retrieved by the addressee. Once a message is retrieved by the addressee it automatically deletes itself from the ZipLip server 24 hours later.

ZipLip offers the ability to automatically filter and sort e-mail according to any text contained in the "From" line or in the "Subject" line of the message. There is also a system that allows you to block e-mail from specific addresses or domains by adding them to a "red list" or to accept e-mail from only specific addresses by adding these addresses to a "green list."

Finally, ZipLip includes a "Secure Calendar," allowing you to maintain a calendar/planner online, encrypted on the ZipLip server. From an e-security and privacy viewpoint, I don't like the idea of having my personal or business calendar stored online. However, if you are someone who uses an online calendar or daily planner anyway, it makes sense to take advantage of the added security provided by ZipLip's secure calendar.

ZipLip is an excellent service that I highly recommend for anyone using Web-based e-mail. The only thing missing is the ability to send anonymous e-mail. When ZipLip was first established, anonymous e-mail was included, but due to misuse, ZipLip chose to discontinue this portion of its service. If you establish a ZipLip account, ask them to bring back the anonymous remailer service. This would make ZipLip the most complete Web-based e-mail service in the world!

> *"I think Americans should get used to a little lessening of our freedoms."*
>
> —Kay Bailey Hutchison, Senator from Texas, shortly after the bombing of the Federal building in Oklahoma City, OK

Free E-Mail Services

UNENCRYPTED WEB-BASED E-MAIL

There are several Web-based e-mail services available, all of which operate basically the same way. Its main advantage is that it is semi-anonymous; when creating an account you are asked for certain identifying information, but no attempt is made to confirm the validity of the information you provide. Furthermore, Web-based e-mail can be accessed from any computer capable of accessing the Internet. Thus, you may access your e-mail from public libraries, cybercafés, university computer labs, and many other public computer terminals.

Everyone who uses e-mail and is concerned with privacy and security should establish a couple of Web-based e-mail accounts. Some places to establish them are:

Anonymous Mail	**http://anonymous.to**
Apex Mail	**http://www.apexmail.com**
Hotmail	**http://www.hotmail.com**
Net @ddress	**http://www.netaddress.com**
Night Mail	**http://www.nightmail.com**
Mail.Com	**http://www.mail.com**
Yahoo! Mail	**http://www.mail.yahoo.com**

When using Web-based e-mail it is important to remember that many of these systems transmit your IP address with your messages. Even those systems that don't transmit your IP address are likely to archive it in order to be able to respond to abuses of their system and violations of their terms of service.

For greatest anonymity when using Web-based e-mail you must access the account from a public terminal (library or cybercafé) where you are not required to sign in or provide other forms of identification to get online.

"Put your trust in God, but mind to keep your powder dry."
—Oliver Cromwell

JUNO

Juno (**http://www.juno.com**) is a great service for someone who simply wants basic e-mail. Juno provides basic e-mail service for free or enhanced e-mail and full Internet access for a nominal fee.

To use Juno you must first obtain a copy of the Juno application software, which can be downloaded from the Juno Web site or mailed to you on a CD by writing to Juno, 1400 E. Lackawanna Avenue, Olyphany, PA 18448. Once you've installed the software on your computer, simply dial in to a local Juno service number for free e-mail. Juno allows those who have no access to the Internet—and thus no access to Web-based e-mail—to still get basic e-mail.

When using Juno's free service you will be regularly presented with offers to upgrade your service to enhanced e-mail or full Internet access, and Juno does provide a good service at slightly less cost than other ISPs. Once you have Juno set up on your computer it is possible to temporarily get rid of the advertisements by going to your "Program Files" folder, then to "Juno," and deleting the "Ads" folder. Juno replaces this folder the next time you log on, but deleting the folder limits the number of advertisements downloaded and makes Juno's free e-mail service quite fast and efficient, at least until the Ads folder is built back up.

Chapter 4

Remailers

> "To consider the judges as the ultimate arbiters of all constitutional questions is a very dangerous doctrine indeed, and one which would place us under the despotism of an oligarchy."
> —Thomas Jefferson

Remailers started back in the early 1990s with what is perhaps the most famous remailer of all, Anon.Penet.Fi, run by Johan Helsingius of Oy Penetic Ab in Finland. The whole idea of Anon.Penet.Fi was that individuals should be able to express themselves freely and with a degree of privacy on the Internet. Helsingius pointed out that to be able to speak freely, without fear of reprisals, you must be able to speak with anonymity.

Unfortunately, Anon.Penet.Fi was brought to an end when the District Court of Helsinki ordered Helsingius to reveal a user's identity after the Church of Scientology claimed the user was posting its copyrighted information to Internet discussion groups through Anon.Penet.Fi.

The fact that Helsingius could turn over the true e-mail address of the individual as ordered by the district court resulted from the fact that Anon.Penet.Fi operated as a pseudo-anonymous server (or Nym-Server) that allowed two-way communication.

A remailer is a program designed to allow you to send anonymous e-mail and make anonymous postings to news groups. A remailer will take any properly formatted e-mail message, remove its identifying header information, and pass the message along to a designated address.

There are several reasons you might want to send anonymous e-mail, but perhaps the most important reason—and here is where remailers perform a great public service—is to allow you to express an opinion about an unpopular topic, in a public forum, without fear of reprisals.

Another important function of remailers is that they provide a countermeasure against communications traffic-pattern analysis. If you are using PGP to encrypt all of your e-mail (and you should be), it will be impossible for anyone monitoring your e-mail to read the content of your messages. However, it may still be possible for someone to develop information about you by monitoring the addresses to which you send and from which you receive e-mail. If you and I were to exchange e-mail messages two or three times per week, it would be clear that we had an ongoing communication about something, even if the content of that communication could not be determined. By properly using remailers you can prevent anyone from determining that we have any type of association, because there is never any direct contact between us!

There are several remailers operating on the Internet at any one time. Some have been around for quite a while and will likely remain in service for a long time, while others come and go fairly quickly. Below is a list of remailers operating during the time this book was being written. Each of the remailers listed had a reliability factor of greater than 90 percent. There are other remailers available, but any remailer operating with less than 90-percent reliability cannot be counted on to deliver your e-mail. To get a current list of remailers check the remailer list maintained by Electronic Frontiers Georgia (EFGA) at **http://anon.efga.org/Remailers/**. The EFGA remailer list is

Remailers

updated every day, so you can always obtain the most current list of remailers and their current reliability. You can also get a list of current remailers from the Publius site at **http://www.publius.net/rlist.html**.

REMAILER NAMES	REMAILER ADDRESSES
squirrel	**mix@squirrel.owl.de**
swiss	**mix@remailer.ch**
hyper2	**mix@hyperreal.art.pl**
lcs	**mix@anon.lcs.mit.edu**
bpm	**remailer@bpm.ai**
widow	**widow@wol.be**
mccain	**mccain@notatla.demon.co.uk**
passthru	
	mixer@immd1.informatik.uni-erlangen.de
nitemare	**nightmare@uni-muenster.de**
teatwo	**teatwo@notatla.demon.co.uk**
hr13	**remailer@hr13.zedz.net**
privacy	**remailer@privacy.nb.ca**

Remailers all use the same basic commands:

anon-to:	Anonymous remailing
anon-post-to:	Anonymous posting to news groups.
cutmarks:	Discards everything below the designated line
encrypted: PGP	Tells remailer it must decrypt PGP message
encrypt-key:	Encrypts message with PGP conventional encryption
latent-time:	Allows time delays to be programmed into message
# #	Pastes new header to remailed message
null	Instructs the remailer to discard the message

To send an anonymous e-mail message you must send a properly formatted message to a remailer. The message will be sent from your e-mail account to the remailer. As an example:

From: **you@your.e-mail.account**
To: **mix@remailer.ch**

On the first line of the body of the message you print two colons (::). On the next line you print the remailer command "anon-to:" followed by the e-mail address where you want the anonymous message delivered. For example:

::
anon-to: **someone@his.e-mail.account**

Skip the next line and then type the text of your message. When the remailer receives your message it removes the header information from your message and forwards the message on to the address on the "anon-to:" line.

Because remailers remove the header information from messages they receive for remailing, they also delete the subject line of the message. If you want to add a subject line to your message you can do this by using the # # remailer command and placing a subject on the following line. For example:
# #
Subject: This Is An Anonymous E-mail Message

One problem encountered when sending anonymous e-mail is that some mail accounts insert a signature file at the bottom of each e-mail message. For example, if you send a message from a Hotmail account, Hotmail adds the following signature file to each message sent:

Remailers

> **Get Your Private, Free Email at http://www.hotmail.com**

And from Yahoo! Mail we get:

> **Do You Yahoo!?**
> **Bid and sell for free at http://auctions.yahoo.com**

Now in regular e-mail this is not a problem, but when appended to an anonymous e-mail message it provides a major clue about where the message came from. Fortunately, remailers solve this problem with the cutmarks: command. By using cutmarks you instruct the remailer to remove everything from any line beginning with the same symbols used at the cutmarks command and everything thereafter. In this example, two dashes were chosen as the symbols:

cutmarks: --
This line will be included in your anonymous e-mail message.
--
This line will be deleted because it follows the cutmarks.

You may want to delay a message for a certain amount of time before you have it delivered by the anonymous remailer. This prevents someone from comparing the times you are logged in to your e-mail server with the times anonymous mail is received by someone else. It also lets you delay messages in order to be somewhere else when the message is received. To delay the delivery of a message from a remailer, use the latent-time: command. For example:

latent-time: +3:00

This will delay the delivery of your message from the remailer for three hours from the time it is received at the remailer. It is also possible to add a random factor to the latent-time command by using the letter "r" after the time. (latent-time: +3:00r). This would deliver the message at some random time after it was received by the remailer, but would not delay more than the indicated three hours.

OK, let's take a look at a properly formatted remailer message using the various remailer commands we have discussed so far.

From: **you@your.e-mail.account**
To: **mix@remailer.ch**
::
anon-to: **someone@his.e-mail.account**
cutmarks: --
latent-time: +3:00
##
Subject: Anonymous Mail

This is the text of your anonymous e-mail message. It will be delayed for three hours from the time it is received by the remailer until it is forwarded to **someone@his.e-mail.account**. *Remember to skip one line between the remailer commands and the body of your message.*
--
This text is below the cut marks and will be deleted from the remailed message.

Most remailers support the use of PGP encryption to further increase the security and anonymity of your e-mail communications. This ensures that even if someone is monitoring e-mail as it leaves your computer, it will be impossible for him to determine the content of your message or to whom it is being sent because the message is encrypted when sent to the remailer. To use the PGP encryption you must, of course, have PGP available on your computer. Then simply prepare your message to be sent through the remailer, as explained above. After your message is properly prepared, encrypt it with the remailer's PGP public key.

Remailers

Type the encrypted PGP command into your e-mail text window and paste your encrypted message below it.
::
Encrypted: PGP
-----BEGIN PGP MESSAGE-----
Version: 2.6.2

pgAAAUiCf6vO7o3XJyAGozxvHW6j14ytQfM8pgNAZ8i6w
PMPUpGQGjV3zEpckW3krlo0iE1xVrMzHEN/tGrbEeZmYGbhR
OQEenIpTQSdlFtVpNdU6gNQI3vacTBujhFXyOhQjOnlBefC1Z
anbrz3bIZJjTpZxOZZemRy4IsABC1QjvJERFTDWj79k0KHwxl5
Armj93MbbHo4byEqRGdvSx680Pkl3vFY4F3493D79P7RZxYZ
h2lfwlKMIsME/+pxQOYWNB8Az+Hq8Ei6Muzst0yic7nwCudY
/imy3n2l/sjx/l8QfnidkeRMv+WCb7z2zsXkiViAE3b+3WsFSmxJ
eTYLHEIsay6Jw0EZaMajNF6qUTNviec9ze7ED168+ifbN6PxkC
o2cJ1pBetXOI0X+QRO3FAR4ygU3kYNrm55owFehT+y03Pd+
pLS9r2r
=zMT8
-----END PGP MESSAGE-----

Because you have encrypted your message prior to sending it, the only thing anyone would see should he intercept your e-mail is unreadable text. When the remailer receives your message, it recognizes the "encrypted: PGP" command and knows the message is encrypted with the remailer's own PGP public key. The remailer then decrypts the message and follows the instructions, as if the message had been sent without encryption. Because the Encrypted: PGP function does so much to enhance security of remailed messages, some remailers (such as Squirrel) will only accept messages encrypted with PGP.

One other thing you can do with PGP and remailers is to use the "encrypt-key" command to have the remailer encrypt a message (or a portion of a message) using PGP's conventional encryption function before forwarding the message. The primary use I have found for the encrypt-key: command is for sending a message from a computer that does not have PGP installed to a computer that has PGP.

For example, you are away on a trip and have information that you need to send securely to a friend. Now, if you were at home you would simply encrypt the message using your friend's PGP public key and send him the message (maybe using a remailer for greater security). But even though you don't have access to your own computer, you do have Internet access and a couple of Web-based e-mail accounts set up (or you could establish one for this one-time use).

To use the encrypt-key: function, prepare your message to be sent through a remailer. After the anon-to: line add the encrypt-key: command followed by the conventional passphrase for this message. Add two asterisks (**) to the following line and then add the text of your message.

From: **you@your.e-mail.account**
To: **mix@remailer.ch**
::

anon-to: **someone@his.e-mail.account**
encrypt-key: Our-Secret-Key
**
*This text will be encrypted using PGP conventional encryption and forwarded anonymously to the recipient of this message (***someone@his.e-mail.account***).*

When the message is received, the recipient will use PGP to decrypt and read this message by typing in the encrypt key for this message (in this case "Our-Secret-Key"). It is important to remember to arrange a conventional passphrase with friends prior to using this technique. If one does not know the passphrase for this specific message, it will be impossible to decrypt and read it.

As we saw when discussing the Anon.Penet.Fi remailer, police or government agencies may bring enough pressure on the administrator of a remailer to cause him to divulge information about you. We can solve the problem of government agencies bringing pressure on remailer administrators by using PGP, and by chaining remailers so that our message passes through more than one before it is sent to the intended recipient.

Looking at the remailer list, we can see that remailers are located in several different countries. Hyper2 is located in Poland, Squirrel is located in Germany, Widow in Belgium, TeaTwo in the United Kingdom, and Swiss, as the name implies, in Switzerland. By chaining remailers we can prevent any single government from being able to track and read our message.

To chain remailers simply prepare the message as if you were going to send it through just a single remailer. Then insert remailer addresses above the address of the final recipient. In the example below we start with the Swiss remailer, which forwards our message to Widow in Belgium. Widow forwards our message to Hyper2 in Poland, which forwards our message to its intended recipient, **someone@his.e-mail.account**.

From: **you@your.e-mail.account**
To: **mix@remailer.ch**
::
anon-to: **widow@wol.be**

::
anon-to: **mix@hyperreal.art.pl**

::
anon-to: **someone@his.e-mail.account**

##
Subject: Anonymous Mail

This anonymous mail has been sent through several remailers, all in separate countries.

The Complete Guide to E-Security

You can add PGP encryption to any or all of the links in the remailer chain, and if the final recipient of your message also has PGP you can encrypt the text of the message with his PGP public key, thereby ensuring that no one other than the intended recipient can read the message at any point along the way.

You should now have a basic understanding of how remailers work. You can practice using remailers by sending messages to yourself through a remailer. The message will go out from your e-mail account, be anonymized and returned to you. Just put your own e-mail address on the "anon-to:" line.

Finally, should you need more information or help getting a specific remailer to work, simply send a blank message to the remailer with "Remailer-Help" on the subject line. The remailer will return its help file to you.

Chapter 5

Understanding Encryption

"No one shall be subjected to arbitrary interference with his privacy, family, home, or correspondence..."
—Article 12, Universal Declaration of Human Rights

To understand e-security it is important to have a basic understanding of encryption. The strength of encryption is primarily a function of the algorithms and formulae used to manipulate the plaintext of your message and the length of the keys.

Simply put, encryption is the manipulation of plaintext characters by a pre-determined method, which thereafter renders the text unintelligible. Encryption ciphers may be categorized as either transposition or substitution. All encryption uses either transposition or substitution ciphers, or a combination of the two.

First, let's take a look at a simple transposition cipher. Starting with the plaintext words "Electronic Security," we can transpose the letter order to get the following encrypted text: EET OIS CRT LCR NCE UIY. This is accomplished by simply placing every other letter of the plaintext on alternating lines.

The Complete Guide to E-Security

E   E   T   O   I   S   C   R   T
   L   C   R   N   C   E   U   I   Y

Now copy the letters from the first line, followed by letters from the second line, and divide them into 3-letter groups. This is a very old method called the "Rail Fence Cipher." As you can see, the letters of the plaintext are all present; they are just in an order that makes no sense to someone trying to read the message.

A substitution cipher replaces the letters of the plaintext with some other character or symbol. Let's start again with our plaintext: "Electronic Security." But now we establish a key allowing us to substitute one letter for another.

Plaintext Alphabet
   A B C D E F G H I J K L M N O P Q R S T U V W X Y Z
Key Alphabet
   B L A C K H O R S E D F G I J M N P Q T U V W X Y Z

Substituting the letters in the words "Electronic Security" from the plaintext alphabet with those of the key alphabet below them, we get the following encrypted text: KFK ATP JIS AQK AUP STY.

Both the transposition and substitution cipher shown above are very easy to break, although they were both used at one time to secure important messages and were perhaps effective enough in their day. Today this type of encryption is often found in children's books or as games in the comic section of the Sunday newspaper. The weakness of both the transposition and substitution ciphers above is not in the methods used for encryption but in the extreme simplicity of algorithm, or formula, used.

An algorithm is nothing more than a set of rules for solving a problem in a finite number of steps. When dealing with encryption an algorithm is simply the set of rules that determine the method for making a given plaintext message unintelligible (encrypting it) and taking the encrypted text and returning it to

Understanding Encryption

its original format (decrypting it). The algorithms used in encryption tend to be very complex mathematical formulae. These algorithms lie at the heart of the cryptographer's art and are the basis for encryption used in e-security. There is any number of algorithms available, some being very useful for encryption, and others being less so.

Algorithms that are available for public examination (such as Diffie-Hellman, RSA, Blowfish, etc.) and can be tested to find their strengths and weaknesses should generally be considered more secure than proprietary algorithms or systems for which the source code is classified (such as Skip Jack).

The browser on your computer likely has some built-in SSL encryption that is used when viewing secure Web sites and transmitting information securely over these connections. The ciphers most commonly used in SSL encryption are

RC4 Cipher	128-bit key
RC2 Cipher	128-bit key
Triple-DES	168-bit key
IDEA	128-bit key
DES	56-bit key
RC4 Export Cipher	40-bit key
RC2 Export Cipher	40-bit key

You can check the strength of your browser's encryption at various sites online, such as **http://www.fortify.net**. You should be using a 128-bit key at the least (it is considered strong encryption and is the current standard). If not, you should immediately upgrade your security by downloading a patch to upgrade to a 128-bit key. These upgrades are generally available free, so there is no reason not to do it. Furthermore, some secure Web sites and online commerce will not accept the older 56- and 40-bit encryption anymore, so it pays to upgrade if you want to use these online services.

When discussing SSL encryption we are discussing symmetric, or single-key, encryption. When we look at programs such as PGP we will see 1,024-bit keys and greater. (This does not mean that PGP is using a key that is 8 times stronger than SSL.) PGP uses asymmetric, or public-key, encryption. The strength of a 128-bit symmetric key and a 1,024-bit asymmetric key are roughly the same.

I mentioned symmetric and asymmetric encryption, which may require brief explanation. Traditionally, encryption methods have been symmetric, or single-key methods. This means that we use one key (or specific set of instructions) to encrypt a message, and the same key allows us to decrypt the message, usually by reversing the encryption process. Symmetric encryption can be very strong and is generally seen to be faster than asymmetric encryption, but there is a problem with it. With symmetric encryption, if the key is compromised the encryption method fails. In order to change keys or to provide new users with encryption keys, there must be a secure method of transmitting these keys. Now, if you already have a secure method of transmitting your symmetric encryption keys, why not just send your messages using the same method? If you don't have a secure method of transmitting your symmetric encryption keys, you run the risk of having your whole system compromised if your key is intercepted when it is sent by a nonsecure means. Key transmission has always been the major weakness of symmetric encryption.

To address the problem of key transmission, cryptographers came up with the process of asymmetric, or public-key encryption. In asymmetric encryption you generate two keys, a public key and a secret key. The public key is used for encryption, but it can't decrypt. It is a one-way or trapdoor algorithm. Processing plaintext with the public key gives an unintelligible encrypted text, but reversing the procedure does not recover the plaintext. In order to decrypt an asymmetrically encrypted message one must have the private key associated with the public key used to encrypt the message in the first place. The advantage of asym-

Understanding Encryption

metric encryption is that there is no longer any problem of finding a secure means of transmitting an encryption key because the public key does not need to be protected. The most commonly available asymmetric encryption system today is PGP, which is freely available on the Internet.

The question that always seems to come up when discussing encryption is: "Can my encryption method be broken?" The answer to this question, quite simply, is YES! Any encryption method can be broken given enough time, effort, money, skill, advances in technology, and luck. The question you should ask is: "Do those who have an interest in breaking my encryption have sufficient time, desire, money, skill, technology, and luck to do so?" Obviously, the simple Rail Fence Cipher could be broken by most anyone with an interest in doing so. High-level encryption methods may be, for all practical purposes, unbreakable given the capabilities of those attempting to break them. However, it is important to remember that what seems to be a high-level encryption method today may become an example of cryptographic failure tomorrow.

The DES 56-bit key and the RSA 512-bit key have been cracked by various teams of cryptanalysts and mathematicians by using the computing power of several computers linked together for that purpose. In one example it took three months to crack an RSA 512-bit key. The total processing power required to crack this one key was about 8,000 MIPS years. (MIPS is millions of instructions per second, so 8,000 MIPS years translates to 8,000 years of computing time for a single computer running 8,000 instructions per second.)

If we compare 128-bit SSL encryption we see that each additional bit added to the key results in a two-fold increase in computation necessary to defeat the key by brute force. A 128-bit key is 7.2×10 to the 16th power more complex than a 56-bit key. Therefore, we can see that even if we had a computer operating at 1 billion MIPS it would require 5.76×10 to the

The Complete Guide to E-Security

14th power years to defeat the 128-bit key by brute force. Simply put, a 128-bit key cannot be defeated by brute-force attack against its algorithm with today's technology.

Since attacking established and tested algorithms is very unlikely to be successful, most attacks against encryption will focus on defeating the passwords used to access the encryption itself. Therefore, ensure that your passwords are strong.

Chapter 6

PGP and Digital Certificates

"It's dangerous to be right when the government is wrong."
—Voltaire

PGP

PGP is an e-mail encryption program created by Phil Zimmermann back in the mid-1980s and released in 1991. Since its invention, PGP has been continually improved upon, becoming more and more user-friendly and incorporating additional features to further enhance the security of your online communications. PGP is arguably the greatest single resource for individual privacy and communications security in the past several years, and anyone who cares at all about privacy and personal freedoms should have PGP installed on his computer.

Finding and Installing PGP

One source for PGP is Zedz Consultants in the Netherlands. You can download PGP from the Zedz Consultants Web site at **http://www.zedz.net.** If you live in the United States or

The Complete Guide to E-Security

Canada you can obtain the latest version of PGP from the MIT Distribution Center for PGP at **http://web.mit.edu/network/pgp.html**. PGP is available free from both of these sites.

The best way to download a copy of the program is with a high-speed modem, since PGP 6.0.2 with RSA is 15.3 megabytes in its compressed format. Save the compressed version to a Zip disk or a Read-Write CD and share this version of PGP with friends and associates who don't have high-speed modems. Once everyone has obtained a compatible version of PGP and installed it on their computers, you can begin sending messages, securely encrypted and safe from prying eyes. Once you have downloaded a copy of PGP it will be necessary to install it on your computer, just like any other type of new software you may obtain. The current versions of PGP can be installed automatically, simply by clicking on the "Set-Up" icon.

During set-up you will be asked to provide a name for the public/private key pair that will be created. You will also be asked to provide an e-mail address to associate with your public key. PGP works just fine without this e-mail address, so you could just leave the field blank. If you choose to have an e-mail address associated with your public key, I recommend that you use one from a Web-based e-mail account such as Hotmail. (The associated e-mail address has no real effect on the public key but is listed after the key name and used as an ID when PGP automatically encrypts messages prior to sending. Since anything you put in the e-mail field during set-up will be listed after the key name, you may use this field for other brief comments associated with your public key, however, this will disable default encryption.)

Finally, you will be asked to provide a passphrase to secure your private key. This should be something you will not forget but that can't be guessed easily by others. The passphrase provides security for your private key. (See the Effective Use of Passwords section in Chapter 2.) PGP will now run through its install/set-up functions and create your public/private key pair.

The key pair created during set-up of PGP (or by using the

PGP and Digital Certificates

"new key" command if PGP is already installed on your computer) consists of a public key used for encrypting and a private, or secret, key used for decrypting. PGP keys look similar to PGP encrypted messages and are stored in a file called a keyring. You will have one keyring for public keys and a second keyring for your private key. You should make your PGP public key generally available. You will give it to anyone with whom you want to communicate securely, as well as posting it to PGP key servers, and perhaps on your Web site. Below is a copy of a PGP public key block. This is what you will provide to other PGP users with whom you communicate. Although the public key looks like a bunch of random gibberish, the PGP program installed on your computer understands the key and uses it when encrypting messages to the key's owner.

----BEGIN PGP PUBLIC KEY BLOCK----
Version: PGP 6.0.2

mQCNAzKsgVYAAAEEAMn+7C1dhC2i/DU6DFiRpklT7iJ
Z7+KjzuQOrlJ1lenBCOKJ
oCQHyeIWgoNMOpJGI6maXbBODuayty71KDYcQfstcjFoP
17hf6zA6mzOykwU1c8S
z4aTM3ie6uhEHtEaH/zxw3CrxfTGYJ0yjw892bfqYmJHBdR
hNcpd/3RXFvEZAAUR
tBJNaWNoYWVsIEUuIENoZXNicm+JAJUDBRAyrcFJyl3/dF
cW8RkBAXFCA/4iWf51
v8IYFc6aOjlDD8D5zSGIETYs4MU4WDU8tawKCaCBAv+P
UKCzYJa//gpXRLd2zDIm
oP1JHC0JMKTZr0nTUW7rI2ZAtUpQIep3kvjerL5I0KjOmxv
e6oXnWmdxnRrilXV9
vrdmzVhkXyp/obf9CHMffylobvU0xgnASZUziokAPwMFED
aY/tU3JD5ycBpj8hEC
/koAnjhNaQW53TMWiifb8ZyYeBB+Sh4bAJ9UCJsvHYCZ8
FlRrnkJxOFMNcKaLQ==
=fEAE

----END PGP PUBLIC KEY BLOCK----

Anyone who has a copy of your public key and has PGP installed on his computer can send you encrypted messages and files. The public key serves only as an encryption key. It cannot be used to decrypt messages that have been encrypted to you. Even the person who encrypted the message using your public key has no way to decrypt it. Once a message or file is encrypted using your public key it can only be decrypted by using the other half of the key pair, your private key.

Key Safety

Your private key must be kept secret. You must *never* give anyone a copy of your PGP private key! The private key is stored on a secret key ring as part of the PGP program. Access to your private key is controlled by the passphrase that you chose when creating your key pair. Anytime you do anything with PGP that requires use of your private key you will be required to enter your passphrase. Therefore, just as you must never give away your private key, you must also safeguard the passphrase that protects it. Unlike your public key, which you will frequently copy and provide to other people, your private key runs in the background and is only accessed by the PGP program itself. PGP is designed so that you cannot accidentally copy your private key. Anytime you are using functions (such as copy) from your PGP key list you are dealing only with your public key ring.

As you continue to use PGP you will acquire dozens (maybe hundreds) of public keys. You should have the public key of every person with whom you communicate or do business with online. Your secret key ring, however, will only contain the private keys of those key pairs you have created. It may in fact have only your own private key, unless you create more than one key pair.

As an extra security measure, you should keep a backup

PGP and Digital Certificates

copy of your key rings, especially your secret key ring. If you ever lost your private key you would be unable to decrypt any message encrypted with its matching public key. I copy my key rings onto a floppy disk, and then encrypt them using PGP's conventional (symmetric) encryption function. Thus, if my computer ever crashes and I lose the key rings on my hard drive, I have a backup and can reinstall the key rings once I repair my system and get a new copy of PGP. However, if the disk containing my backup key rings was ever stolen it would be useless to the thief because the information is protected with PGP's conventional encryption.

Types of PGP

There are several versions of PGP available. These different versions represent upgrades in PGP, as well as different packages for PGP depending on whether it will be used for business or personal correspondence.

The initial versions of PGP used the RSA algorithm (named for inventors Ron Rivest, Adi Shamir, and Leonard Adleman) as the basis for its encryption. Current versions of PGP (5.0 and later) use the algorithm developed in 1975 by Whitfield Diffie and Martin Hellman. The primary reason for this change was that there is a copyright on RSA, while the Diffie-Hellman algorithm is in the public domain. Both algorithms provide for excellent security, so the change did not in any way weaken the security of a message encrypted with PGP. There is, however, a problem: the RSA and Diffie-Hellman algorithms are not cross-compatible. What this means to you is that if you use a later version of PGP (with the Diffie-Hellman algorithm) to encrypt a message and send it to someone using an earlier version of PGP (with the RSA algorithm), the message can't be decrypted.

This problem of compatibility has been addressed to some extent by including RSA in some of the later versions of PGP, thus allowing use of both RSA and Diffie-Hellman keys. When getting your copy of PGP, try to get a copy that contains both algorithms. Current versions also integrate seamlessly with Windows 95/98, allowing you to encrypt and decrypt messages by copying and pasting them from the clipboard, as well as work with entire files using Windows Explorer. The earlier versions of PGP will accomplish the same functions but require greater effort and working from the command line or the use of an additional Windows interface.

This is an example of a PGP encrypted message:

-----BEGIN PGP MESSAGE-----
Version: PGP 6.0.2

qANQR1DBwU4D9MvK736h0lsQCADLd6SO6bIqz7rkGp1b3aBraEwCr9KPNY2e4rvu
FEsDo+oR5mwu0vaglqr0vDrJYLjW1TCp8+VrdmNYZ5ew4U1ndMfS9VIoQWtDcPye
AzJx1GzgCeBGqSxHjsOn2xZwZBDIAU4fkpJhpHU7rx+daEtLHGBDHrwd7Ng2n6ck
xbbWO2tS2vLdpmpVjGRxXMlOiFhVPmnsa3NkO6qBV4hcDlcBL3SMmcY8AHebWsRO
=ZFrS
-----END PGP MESSAGE-----

Using PGP

Once you have PGP installed on your computer, you should use it regularly in all your e-mail communications, encouraging everyone with whom you have e-mail communication to get and use it. It should not be unusual for there to be PGP-encrypted messages being sent from and received at your e-mail account. Since its release in 1991, PGP has become the unofficial standard for secure e-mail on the Internet. PGP-encrypted e-mail draws no particular attention to itself, and the more commonly it is used, the less likely it will be that encryption will raise any flags with Big Brother.

Most everyone with whom I communicate via e-mail uses

PGP and Digital Certificates

PGP. My PGP public key is available on various key servers online, thus making it fairly easy to obtain a copy. Some places to post your public key and search for the public keys of others are:

BAL's PGP Public Key Server
http://pgp5.ai.mit.edu
Open Key Server
http://www.keyserver.net
PGP Server at ETH Zurich
http://www.tik.ee.ethz.ch/~pgp
University of Paderborn, Germany
http://math-www.uni-paderborn.de/pgp/

Fingerprints

As we saw with e-mail traps—creating a fake e-mail address and pretending to be someone else—it is also possible to create a PGP encryption key that has a misleading identifier. You can name your public key anything that you want to, even exactly copying the name of another public key. The key itself will be different, but the key name can be the same as another. PGP solves the problem of fake keys with key fingerprints.

When I provide my e-mail address to someone, I also provide him with a copy of my PGP-key fingerprint—a series of letters and numbers that form a fingerprint or serial number for each key. (As an example, the key fingerprint for my actual PGP public key is: 2BD5 F827 1221 BC4A C877 F38F 3724 3E72 701A 63F2.) If you were to receive a PGP public key (or find it posted on a key server or Web page) that purported to be Michael Edward Chesbro's PGP public key, you need only compare the key fingerprints to be sure. If the key fingerprints do not match, the key is not mine. When you create your PGP keys, the fingerprint is automatically generated and included in the key-properties listing. It requires no extra steps or download. Think of the key fingerprint as a serial number for your PGP key. It allows you to quickly identify a particular key without trying to compare the entire key format and also lets you provide key confirmation by a separate communication channel (such as reading the fingerprint over the telephone).

Conventional Encryption

PGP will also allow you to encrypt messages using conventional or single-key encryption (the same key is used to encrypt and to decrypt). For regular communication between individuals using PGP, I don't see a lot of value to conventional encryption, as public key encryption offers greater security. However, I have found a very useful function for conventional encryption—the dissemination of information among a large group of individuals who may not communicate regularly or even know each other. For example, a group may wish to produce an electronic newsletter exclusively for members of the group. The newsletter is encrypted using PGP conventional encryption and sent via e-mail to the subscribers. Once the encrypted newsletter is received, the recipient must know the conventional passphrase for that newsletter in order to decrypt and read it. The encrypted newsletter could even be posted to a Web site, or made available on a bulletin board system (BBS) or via file transfer protocol (FTP). Anyone could obtain a copy of the encrypted newsletter, but unless he knew the passphrase associated with the newsletter he could never read it.

Digital Signatures

Another security feature offered by PGP is the digital signature. While a man's handwritten signature is often accepted as proof that he has authored, read, or approved of a document, a handwritten signature cannot simply be attached to e-mail or other electronically transmitted messages. Even if a graphic image of one's signature were to be attached it would be easy to alter the text above the signature or copy the signature and append it to other messages. Digital signatures—strings of letters and num-

PGP and Digital Certificates

bers—prevent electronic documents from being altered without destroying the validity of the signature.

—--BEGIN PGP SIGNED MESSAGE—--
Hash: SHA1
When you sign a message with your digital signature, PGP will use your private key and require you to enter your passphrase in order to develop the signature. This provides strong evidence that you did in fact sign the document in question. After all, you do protect your private key and never tell anyone your passphrase, right? Without your PGP private key and knowledge of your passphrase, a digital signature cannot be generated. As you can see, I have added my digital signature to this paragraph:

—--BEGIN PGP SIGNATURE—--
Version: PGP 6.0.2
iQA/AwUBODl76TckPnJwGmPyEQLejwCgh0AErtR9XIvIk
RqmFBRpxl7aalUAoNg7
jFB1iTtVfdDRv5zc6hcn5mLa
=8lmx
—--END PGP SIGNATURE—--

Were I to digitally sign another paragraph, the numbers and letters in my digital signature would be different. The reason for this is that PGP calculates a value for any message to be digitally signed and then uses that value with your private key to create the digital signature. Any change to a digitally signed message (even so minor a change as the addition of a space or changing a capital letter to lowercase) will change the computed value of the message and cause PGP to report a bad signature. Anyone can use PGP with your public key to verify your digital signature. When PGP reports a good signature, you can be certain that what you have received is exactly what was signed and sent by whoever signed that message or file. A good signature also shows the name of the key that produced the digital signature and the date and time the message or file was signed.

Security Questions

The question is often asked, "Just how secure is PGP, anyway?" The answer is no one really knows for sure.

There is a rumor that circulates from time to time concerning PGP 5.0 and beyond regarding PGP changing from RSA to Diffie-Hellman. The rumor is that the government dropped its opposition to PGP following the change to Diffie-Hellman because the government has a way to defeat it, or because Zimmermann incorporated a back door into later versions of PGP, or other such things, all with the supposition that PGP is now severely weakened. I doubt any of these rumors are true.

First, the Diffie-Hellman algorithm has no clearly exploitable weaknesses. Second, the source code for PGP is available to anyone who wants it, thus allowing the private sector to identify weaknesses in the updated versions of PGP. To date no one has come forward with any information identifying back doors or other built-in weaknesses to PGP. Finally, in addition to being available as freeware, PGP is offered in a commercial package. The company offering the commercial version of PGP and the companies buying it to secure their business communications are all going to pay particular attention to the security of this product. To date there have been no claims within the industrial security community, nor any suits filed in the courts claiming that PGP has failed to provide adequate security.

It is interesting to note the comments of Louis J. Freeh, Director of the F.B.I., in a speech he made on July 12, 1999, entitled "Encryption and Electronic Surveillance." Speaking of PGP, Freeh stated, "Now, if you're using this particular software product and your encryption is robust to the level of 120-plus bits, law enforcement would need 280 networked computers working on one particular part of that text, one message unit, and working for 4 trillion times the age of the universe in order to

PGP and Digital Certificates

unscramble it. That means, in effect, we cannot unscramble it."

Based on the evidence at hand, it is reasonable to state that PGP is unbreakable using the current technology and techniques of cryptanalysis. However, it pays to remember that today's unbreakable encryption may be tomorrow's example of weak encryption techniques.

If you paid attention in your high-school history classes you are aware of the German Enigma cipher used during World War II. The Germans believed that the Enigma could not be broken, and for a while they were right. However, cryptoanalists finally found a way to determine a solution for Enigma, and the Allies were thereafter able to read German military traffic encrypted with Enigma almost as quickly as the Germans themselves.

I trust PGP to encrypt my communications and files effectively, and I use a version of PGP that employs the Diffie-Hellman algorithm. (However, it is possible to use RSA if you do not trust Diffie-Hellman, and my version also contains the RSA algorithm, and I have an RSA key that I can use.) There is also the option of double encryption (encrypting a message and then encrypting the encrypted text again). Though I trust PGP, I also understand the fleeting nature of real e-security and continue to check, verify, and employ additional security methodology.

Using PGP to Secure Files

In addition to using PGP to secure your e-mail communications, you can use PGP to secure files stored on your computer. Is there anything on your computer that you would not want read by someone else? Do you manage your personal finances or maintain a diary on your computer? Even if you live alone and believe that no one other than yourself has access to your files, what happens if your computer is stolen? What if, as we saw reported in the *Washington Post,* the Justice Department gains authority to conduct covert actions against American citizens and somehow you become one of the targets of this covert action? Would you want some crook or government agent to be able to read everything on your personal computer?

In current versions of PGP we find something called PGP disk, which allows you to create a secure, encrypted partition on your hard drive. When PGP disk is mounted, you access it like any other disk drive on your system. Once you unmount PGP disk, everything saved to that partition is encrypted and the partition is no longer visible or accessible as a drive.

By using PGP disk you have a secure place to store your sensitive files. Whether you are trying to protect your household budget, personal letters, business plans, or plans to take over the world, PGP disk ensures that even if someone was to gain access to your computer, your private files would remain private.

Even if the version of PGP that you use does not have PGP disk as part of its package, you can still secure files on your computer simply by encrypting the files with your own PGP public key. Should someone gain access to your computer, he would have the encrypted files, and possibly your PGP private key, but without knowledge of your PGP passphrase he still could not decrypt your files.

The point here is to use encryption in all your communications, but do not be deceived into believing that an encrypted message will never be revealed to an enemy! Even the best cipher systems may be broken over time given new advances in technology.

> "Experience should teach us to be most on our guard to protect liberty when the government's purposes are beneficent . . . the greatest dangers to liberty lurk in insidious encroachment by men of zeal, well meaning but without understanding."
>
> —Justice Louis Brandeis,
> Olmstead v. United States Supreme Court, 1928

DIGITAL CERTIFICATES

There may come a time when you find it necessary or desirable to have a process for automatic authentication and encryp-

PGP and Digital Certificates

tion in place on your computer. One method is the use of a digital certificate, which is simply a public key associated with an authenticated identity.

A digital certificate accomplishes two major purposes. First, it provides a public key (encryption key) allowing anyone in receipt of the digital certificate to encrypt messages to the owner of that certificate. Second, it provides, to some degree, evidence that the owner of the digital certificate is who he claims to be.

A digital certificate is issued by a trusted third party, called a Certificate Authority (CA). The major CAs are

VeriSign	**http://www.verisign.com**
Thawte	**http://www.thawte.com**
GlobalSign	**http://www.globalsign.net**

There are several other CAs, but in my opinion these are the top three. Almost anyone can issue a digital certificate, and some companies and organizations will issue their own digital certificates to their employees or members to establish their own internal Web-of-trust. The validity of the authentication of the digital certificate comes down to just how much you trust the CA to confirm identities.

Each company may ask for slightly different information, but basically they all require sufficient information to establish positive identification of the individual or business requesting digital certification. Assuming you wanted to obtain a personal digital certificate from Thawte, you would be required to provide the following information: your identification number, passport number, Social Security number, driver's license number, or tax number (depending on your nationality); your full name and date of birth; your employer's name (if you are employed), size of the company, and address; your home address and contact details; and your preferred currency.

Once you have provided Thawte with this information, they

will establish a Thawte ID number for you, which will look something like this: US-123456789-1. In the United States the center number (123456789) would be your Social Security number. (While it is bad practice to use your Social Security number for ID purposes, as detailed in *Privacy for Sale*, it is necessary here.) In other countries it would be some other form of national ID number, such as your passport number. You will use this number to communicate with Thawte and be issued a personal digital certificate.

In addition to the above requested information, you usually have to pay a small fee for the digital certificate (at the time of this writing VeriSign charged about $15 per year). This payment is usually made by credit card or by a direct debit from your bank account, thus providing even more information about you that will be stored in the CA's database and associated with your digital certificate.

After providing the information and paying the fee, you will be issued a digital certificate by the CA. Your digital certificate contains a public key for you and is signed by the CA with its private key, thereby establishing the validity of your digital certificate. You are also provided with a root certificate, which is nothing more than the CA's public key, which allows you to verify the validity of the CA's signature on the digital certificates it issues.

Installing the root certificate and your personal digital certificate on your computer is a fairly simple matter, and instructions for installation are included with most certificates issued. (Installation varies slightly depending on the system you are using, but it is pretty much double-click and follow the onscreen instructions.) However, you must be using Netscape (Netscape Communicator) or MicroSoft IE (Outlook or Outlook Express) in order to use a personal digital certificate. If you are using some other software to access the Internet and send e-mail (AOL, Juno, etc.), there may be no way to install your digital certificate.

Once installed you can sign messages you send using your digital certificate, thus allowing the recipient to be sure the mes-

PGP and Digital Certificates

sage has not been tampered with. You can also include a copy of your digital certificate in your messages, allowing the recipient of your message to maintain a copy of your digital certificate to use in encrypting messages he sends to you. (Remember, your digital certificate is a public key.) Finally, you can use your digital certificate to identify yourself to various membership-based servers that connect via a secure connection.

After you have installed your digital certificate on your system, you can generally set your security protocols to automatically sign any messages you send and encrypt messages to anyone whose digital certificate you possess.

Digital certificates clearly have their place and are definitely a benefit when dealing with online businesses; however, I am not really a fan of them for personal use. I believe that the amount of information demanded by the major CAs is simply too intrusive. You can establish a level of trust and authentication and send encrypted messages using such programs as PGP without having to disclose personal information to a third party CA.

For those who are interested in adding a digital certificate to their e-security plan but are unwilling to disclose the information required by the major CAs, there is another option. Various groups will provide digital certificates anonymously and without a fee to whoever requests them. A couple of places you may obtain an anonymous digital certificate are: PrivacyX (**http://www.privacyx.com**) and WildID (**http://www.wildid.com**). Like the major CAs, these companies provide the root certificate and personal digital certificate, but they require no identifying information beyond a name/pseudonym and an e-mail address to issue the digital certificate.

Once you have installed your digital certificate from PrivacyX, WildID, or other like companies you have all the same signing and encryption features provided by the major CAs without the associated disclosure of personal information.

Of course, the advantage of a digital certificate without the requirement for disclosing personal information may become a serious detriment if you are relying on the digital certificate as the sole means of authentication and identification of an online associate. If you are using one of these nonvalidated digital certificates, be sure that you do your own validation on any certificates you receive from other people before trusting them. Also, be prepared to provide a way for those relying on your digital certificate to authenticate that you are who and what you claim to be.

The bottom line regarding digital certificates is this: If you own a business or are conducting business online, get and use a digital certificate from one of the major CAs. If you simply need a method for encrypting and authenticating e-mail among a small group of friends and colleagues, use one of the anonymous digital certificates and validate the trust of the certificate yourself using a separate means.

Chapter 7

One-Time Pads

"Rebellion to tyrants is obedience to God."
—Thomas Jefferson

Communication security is an essential element for anyone trying to protect his privacy and personal freedoms. Although the best systems for maintaining the security of your communications use computer-generated, high-level encryption schemes (such as PGP), you may not always have access to a computer or may only have access to one without encryption and other security programs installed. In cases such as this, you must use a manual system.

There are several systems available, all of which provide some degree of security. The problem with many of these manual systems is that the degree of security offered is simply not sufficient to protect your messages from cryptanalysis. As children we perhaps played with simple substitution ciphers (A=1, B=2, C=3, etc.). You may find this same type of cipher located with the crossword puzzle and comics in your daily newspaper. Clearly something this simple should not be used to secure sensitive messages. Other systems, such as transposition ciphers, grids, and more complex substitution

The Complete Guide to E-Security

ciphers, are also all quite easily cracked with basic cryptanalysis. There is, however, a system that is not vulnerable to basic cryptanalysis—the one-time pad.

In 1917, the United States was engaged in World War I and needed a cipher system that couldn't be broken by the Central Powers. Maj. Joseph O. Mauborgne, (later major general and 12th chief signal officer) turned to Gilbert Vernam at American Telephone and Telegraph (AT&T). Vernam's response was the one-time pad, a system that was not broken by the Germans during the Great War and hasn't been broken by anyone else to date. The one-time pad provides a cipher system that is, by any practical meaning of the word, unbreakable, *when used correctly*. The thing that makes a one-time pad so secure is that a key is used only once and then destroyed. This gives anyone trying to break the cipher no patterns to analyze, and thus no way to determine the key and decipher the message.

To use one-time pad ciphers you must have a series of random letters or other symbols equal to or longer than the plaintext of your message. These series are recorded on sheets (with several sheets making up a small pad) that are used only once—thus, "one-time pad." A message is encrypted using a sheet from the one-time pad, after which that sheet is destroyed. When the message is received the recipient uses the corresponding sheet from his copy of the pad to decrypt the message, then destroys that sheet.

There are many ways to use a one-time pad to encrypt plaintext, but the way I find easiest is with a Vigenere Square, using the one-time pad as an aperiodic key in the polyalphabetic substitution.

For example, if you have the following one-time pad and want to encrypt the word "Privacy," you start by writing the letters of the one-time pad above the letters of the plaintext as in the following example:

```
jebs    jeot    dorp    preg
oprk    ysau    owhk    wnau
ieja    lwhc    ltwu    sxzc

j e b s j e o
p r i v a c y
```

One-Time Pads

Now, using the Vigenere Square, locate the one-time pad key letter in the top row and the plaintext letter in the far left column. Follow the corresponding row and column until they meet. The letter where the row and column meet is the letter of the cipher text. The first letter of the cipher text in this case is "y," because this is where the column that starts with "J" meets the row that starts with "P."

*	A	B	C	D	E	F	G	H	I	J	K	L	M	N	O	P	Q	R	S	T	U	V	W	X	Y	Z
A	a	b	c	d	e	f	g	h	I	j	k	l	m	n	o	p	q	r	s	t	u	v	w	x	y	z
B	b	c	d	e	f	g	h	I	j	k	l	m	n	o	p	q	r	s	t	u	v	w	x	y	z	a
C	c	d	e	f	g	h	I	j	k	l	m	n	o	p	q	r	s	t	u	v	w	x	y	z	a	b
D	d	e	f	g	h	I	j	k	l	m	n	o	p	q	r	s	t	u	v	w	x	y	z	a	b	c
E	e	f	g	h	I	j	k	l	m	n	o	p	q	r	s	t	u	v	w	x	y	z	a	b	c	d
F	f	g	h	I	j	k	l	m	n	o	p	q	r	s	t	u	v	w	x	y	z	a	b	c	d	e
G	g	h	I	j	k	l	m	n	o	p	q	r	s	t	u	v	w	x	y	z	a	b	c	d	e	f
H	h	I	j	k	l	m	n	o	p	q	r	s	t	u	v	w	x	y	z	a	b	c	d	e	f	g
I	I	j	k	l	m	n	o	p	q	r	s	t	u	v	w	x	y	z	a	b	c	d	e	f	g	h
J	j	k	l	m	n	o	p	q	r	s	t	u	v	w	x	y	z	a	b	c	d	e	f	g	h	I
K	k	l	m	n	o	p	q	r	s	t	u	v	w	x	y	z	a	b	c	d	e	f	g	h	I	j
L	l	m	n	o	p	q	r	s	t	u	v	w	x	y	z	a	b	c	d	e	f	g	h	I	j	k
M	m	n	o	p	q	r	s	t	u	v	w	x	y	z	a	b	c	d	e	f	g	h	I	j	k	l
N	n	o	p	q	r	s	t	u	v	w	x	y	z	a	b	c	d	e	f	g	h	I	j	k	l	m
O	o	p	q	r	s	t	u	v	w	x	y	z	a	b	c	d	e	f	g	h	I	j	k	l	m	n
P	p	q	r	s	t	u	v	w	x	y	z	a	b	c	d	e	f	g	h	I	j	k	l	m	n	o
Q	q	r	s	t	u	v	w	x	y	z	a	b	c	d	e	f	g	h	I	j	k	l	m	n	o	p
R	r	s	t	u	v	w	x	y	z	a	b	c	d	e	f	g	h	I	j	k	l	m	n	o	p	q
S	s	t	u	v	w	x	y	z	a	b	c	d	e	f	g	h	I	j	k	l	m	n	o	p	q	r
T	t	u	v	w	x	y	z	a	b	c	d	e	f	g	h	I	j	k	l	m	n	o	p	q	r	s
U	u	v	w	x	y	z	a	b	c	d	e	f	g	h	I	j	k	l	m	n	o	p	q	r	s	t
V	v	w	x	y	z	a	b	c	d	e	f	g	h	I	j	k	l	m	n	o	p	q	r	s	t	u
W	w	x	y	z	a	b	c	d	e	f	g	h	I	j	k	l	m	n	o	p	q	r	s	t	u	v
X	x	y	z	a	b	c	d	e	f	g	h	I	j	k	l	m	n	o	p	q	r	s	t	u	v	w
Y	y	z	a	b	c	d	e	f	g	h	I	j	k	l	m	n	o	p	q	r	s	t	u	v	w	x
Z	z	a	b	c	d	e	f	g	h	I	j	k	l	m	n	o	p	q	r	s	t	u	v	w	x	y

The Complete Guide to E-Security

The next cipher letter is "v," which is where the "E" and "R" column and row meet. You continue this procedure until you have encrypted the entire message. The word "privacy" is encrypted as "yvjnjfm."

To decrypt the message, simply reverse the procedure. Look at the first letter of your one-time pad, which in this case is "J." Follow down the J-column until you come to the cipher text letter (in this case, "y"). The letter to the far left on this row is the first letter of your plaintext, the letter "P." Continue this procedure until you have discovered the plaintext of your message.

This one-time pad method is very secure as long as you never reuse a key from your one-time pad. If you use a key more than once it weakens the system to the point that it is likely that all messages encrypted with the same key can be broken through basic cryptanalysis.

To prepare a one-time pad you must first come up with a series of random letters. Using a computer to generate a random series only creates a pseudorandom series, because the way computers function prevents a true random series. But computer-generated pseudoseries are significantly random to protect most any information from decryption. No individual, private investigator, corporation, law enforcement agency, or the like will be able to break a one-time pad encryption using a pseudorandom key. I suppose that if that National Security Agency (NSA) devoted its massive computing power and cryptanalysis technology to determining the pseudorandom key used to create your one-time pad, it might be done. However, if the NSA is devoting that type of asset to reading your messages you should be more concerned about the 15 guys stacked outside your door at 2 A.M. wearing body armor and face masks and carrying submachine guns.

There are several one-time pad generators available online. One that I like is at the Fourmilab Switzerland Web site at **http://www.fourmilab.ch/onetime/**

Here is a one-time pad generated at the Fourmilab Web site

One-Time Pads

and the associated public domain document on that page that explains how the one-time pad generator works:

One-Time Pad Generator

This page, which requires that your browser support JavaScript (see Why JavaScript below), generates one-time pads or password lists in a variety of forms. It is based on a high-quality pseudorandom sequence generator, which can be seeded either from the current date and time, or from a seed you provide. Fill in the form below to select the format of the pad and press "Generate" to create the pad in the text box. You can then copy and paste the generated pad into another window to use as you wish. Each of the labels on the request form is linked to a description of that parameter.

Output: Number of keys: **50**   Line length: **72**
Format: Key length: **4**   Group length: **8**
Composition: Key text: Numeric
Word-like
             Alphabetic **X** Gibberish Upper case letters
             Random separators   Include signatures
Seed: From clock: **X**   User-defined:

1) spby-mldt 2) saju-uomu 3) pltg-uezg 4) gzlu-tdsp
5) eyhp-kisq 6) olmc-pikd 7) urvp-vdam 8) xarz-rifq
9) qpld-bdvk 10) cwuq-byjr 11) sxhm-etop 12) ixgg-xytn
13) vfmc-gmxa 14) ivte-nygm 15) dubs-urxq 16) dqvg-bkaa
17) uazd-jebz 18) zfyv-daor 19) kbna-qssu 20) ezub-warb
21) tkky-cyek 22) jvvf-ydpe 23) mmmx-rrqp 24) hzir-qrff
25) qujo-dtro 26) yacg-yrvt 27) aomf-axqf 28) dywh-osbr
29) zetx-wbav 30) ydyv-judt 31) hvjq-scqf 32) qqbp-paxj
33) bazp-gknm 34) pmuh-pbnx 35) exyr-gaed 36) epex-tvou
37) pnid-wynn 38) whlo-btko 39) mujg-kwhg 40) mpfh-lyhj
41) ksni-eigh 42) jwme-hcou 43) ftel-vfps 44) shlr-bomv
45) xrdy-ezcx 46) vvhg-xdcq 47) gaav-xoly 48) zuxp-iqzc
49) dumh-cnlj 50) hlls-hbco

Details

Each of the fields in the one-time pad request form is described below.

Output

Number of keys

Enter the number of keys you'd like to generate. If you generate more than fit in the results text box, you can use the scroll bar to view the additional lines.

Line length

Lines in the output will be limited to the given length (or contain only one key if the line length is less than required for a single key). If the line length is greater than the width of the results box, you can use the horizontal scroll bar to view the rest of the line. Enter 0 to force one key per line; this is handy when you're preparing a list of keys to be read by a computer program.

Format

Key length

Each key will contain this number of characters, not counting separators between groups.

Group length

If a nonzero value is entered in this field, the key will be broken into groups of the given number of characters by separators. Humans find it easier to read and remember sequences of characters when divided into groups of five or fewer characters.

Composition

Key text

This set of radio buttons lets you select the character set used in the keys. The alternatives are listed in order of increasing security.

Numeric
Keys contain only the decimal digits "0" through "9." Least secure.

Word-like
Keys are composed of alphabetic characters which obey the digraph statistics of English text. Such keys contain sequences of vowels and consonants familiar to speakers of Western languages, and are therefore usually easier to memorise but, for a given key length, are less secure than purely random letters.

Alphabetic
Keys consist of letters of the alphabet chosen at random. Each character has an equal probability of being one of the 26 letters.

Gibberish
Keys use most of the printable ASCII character set, excluding only characters frequently used for quoting purposes. This option provides the greatest security for a given key length, but most people find keys like this difficult to memorise or even transcribe from a printed pad. If a human is in the loop, it's often better to use a longer alphabetic or word-like key. Most secure.

Uppercase letters
If this box is checked, keys generated with Word-like, Alphabetic, and Gibberish key text will contain only uppercase (capital) letters. Most people find it easier to read lowercase letters than all capitals, but for some applications (for example, where keys must be scanned optically by hardware that only recognises capital letters), capitals are required. Checking this box when Key text is set to Gibberish causes the Gibberish keys to contain only capitals instead of a mix of upper- and lowercase letters; such keys are said to pass the "telephone test": you can read them across a (hopefully secure) voice link without having to indicate whether each letter is or is not a capital.

Random separators

When the Key length is longer than a nonzero Group length specification, the key is divided into sequences of the given group length by separator characters. By default, a hyphen, "-", is used to separate groups. If you check this box, separators will be chosen at random among punctuation marks generally acceptable for applications such as passwords. If you're generating passwords for a computer system, random separators dramatically increase the difficulty of guessing passwords by exhaustive search.

Include signatures

When this box is checked, at the end of the list of keys, preceded by a line beginning with ten dashes "-", the 128 bit MD5 signature of each key is given, one per line, with signatures expressed as 32 hexadecimal digits. Key signatures can be used to increase security when keys are used to control access to computer systems or databases. Instead of storing a copy of the keys, the computer stores their signatures. When the user enters a key, its signature is computed with the same MD5 algorithm used to generate it initially, and the key is accepted only if the signature matches. Since discovering a key which will generate a given signature is believed to be computationally prohibitive, even if the list of signatures stored on the computer is compromised, that information will not permit an intruder to deduce a valid key.

Signature calculation is a computationally intense process for which JavaScript is not ideally suited; be patient while signatures are generated, especially if your computer has modest processing speed.

For signature-based validation to be secure, it is essential the original keys be long enough to prohibit discovery of matching signatures by exhaustive search. Suppose, for example, one used four digit numeric keys, as used for Personal Identification Numbers (PINs) by many credit card systems. Since only 10,000 different keys exist, one could simply compute the signatures of every possible key from 0000 through 9999, permitting an attacker who came into possession of the table of signatures to recover the keys by a simple lookup process. For maxi-

One-Time Pads

mum security, keys must contain at least as much information as the 128-bit signatures computed from them. This implies a minimum key length (not counting non-random separator characters) for the various key formats as follows:

Key Composition	Minimum Characters
Numeric	39
Word-like	30
Alphabetic	28
Gibberish	20

It should be noted that for many practical applications there is no need for anything approaching 128-bit security. The guidelines above apply only in the case where maximum protection in the event of undetected compromise of key signatures occurs. In many cases, much shorter keys are acceptable, especially when it is assumed that a compromise of the system's password or signature database would be only part of a much more serious subversion of all resources on the system.

Seed

The seed is the starting value which determines all subsequent values in the pseudorandom sequence used to generate the one-time pad. Given the seed, the pad can be reproduced. The seed is a 31-bit number which can be derived from the date and time at which the one-time pad was requested or from a user-defined seed value. If the user-defined seed consists entirely of decimal digits, it is used directly as the seed, modulo 231; if a string containing non-digit characters is entered, it is used to compute a hash code which is used to seed the generator.

When the clock is used as the seed, the clock value is entered in the User-defined box to allow you, by checking "User-defined," to produce additional pads with the same seed.

Why JavaScript?

At first glance, JavaScript may seem an odd choice for programming a page such as this. The one-time pad generator program is rather large and complicated, and downloading it to your browser takes longer than would be required for a Java applet or to transfer a one-time pad generated by a CGI program on the Web server. I chose JavaScript for two reasons: security and transparency.

Security

The sole reason for the existence of one-time pads is to provide a source of information known only to people to whom they have been distributed in a secure manner. This means the generation process cannot involve any link whose security is suspect. If the pad were generated on a Web server and transmitted to you, it would have to pass over the Internet, where any intermediate site might make a copy of your pad before you even received it. Even if some mechanism such as encryption could absolutely prevent the pad's being intercepted, you'd still have no way to be sure the site generating the pad didn't keep a copy in a file, conveniently tagged with your Internet address.

In order to have any degree of security, it is essential that the pad be generated on your computer, without involving any transmission or interaction with other sites on the Internet. A Web browser with JavaScript makes this possible, since the generation program embedded in this page runs entirely on your own computer and does not transmit anything over the Internet. Its output appears only in the text box, allowing you to cut and paste it to another application. From there on, its security is up to you.

Security is never absolute. A one-time pad generated with this page might be compromised in a variety of ways, including the following:

- Your Web browser and/or JavaScript interpreter may contain bugs or deliberate security violations which report activity on your computer back to some other Internet site.
- Some other applet running on another page of your browser, perhaps without your being aware of its existence, is spying on other windows.
- Some other application running on your computer may have com-

One-Time Pads

promised your system's security and be snooping on your activity.
- Your Web browser may be keeping a "history log" or "cache" of data you generate. Somebody may come along later and recover a copy of the pad from that log.
- The implementation of this page may contain a bug or deliberate error which makes its output predictable. This is why transparency, discussed below, is essential.
- Your computer's security may have been compromised physically; when's the last time you checked that a bug that transmits your keystrokes and/or screen contents to that white van parked down the street wasn't lurking inside your computer cabinet?

One can whip oneself into a fine fever of paranoia worrying about things like this. One way to rule out the most probable risks is to download a copy of the generator page and run it from a "file:" URL on a computer which has no network connection whatsoever and is located in a secure location under your control. And look very carefully at any files created by your Web browser. You may find the most interesting things squirreled away there. . . .

Transparency

Any security-related tool is only as good as its design and implementation. Transparency means that, in essence, all the moving parts are visible so you can judge for yourself whether the tool merits your confidence. In the case of a program, this means that source code must be available, and that you can verify that the program you're running corresponds to the source code provided.

The very nature of JavaScript achieves this transparency. The program is embedded into this actual Web page; to examine it you need only use your browser's "View Source" facility, or save the page into a file on your computer and read it with a text editor. JavaScript's being an interpreted language eliminates the risk of your running a program different from the purported source code: with an interpreted language what you read is what you run.

Transparency is important even if you don't know enough about

The Complete Guide to E-Security

programming or security to determine whether the program contains any flaws. The very fact that it can be examined by anybody allows those with the required expertise to pass judgement, and you can form your own conclusions based on their analysis.

Credits

The pseudorandom sequence generator is based on L'Ecuyer's two-sequence generator as described in Communications of the ACM, Vol. 31 (1968), page 742. A Bays-Durham shuffle is used to guard against regularities lurking in L'Ecuyer's algorithm; see ACM Transactions on Mathematical Software, Vol. 2 (1976) pages 59-64 for details.

The JavaScript implementation of the MD5 message-digest algorithm was developed by Henri Torgemane; please view the source code for this page to examine the code, including the copyright notice and conditions of use. The MD5 algorithm was developed by Ron Rivest. Additional information regarding MD5 can be found at the RSA Data Security, Inc. site.

---

by John Walker

May 26, 1997

This document is in the public domain.

Chapter 8

Encryption Programs

"Necessity is the plea for every infringement of human freedom. It is the argument of tyrants; it is the creed of slaves."
—William Pitt, before the House of Commons, November 18, 1783

When we consider encryption programs, there seems to be an almost never-ending stream of programs offered by security companies, software companies, students majoring in mathematics or cryptography, and amateur programmers enjoying their hobby and seeing what they can create. Some of these encryption programs are excellent, while others are pure sh . . . let's just say, not so good. The problem is that the average user, needing encryption as part of his e-security planning, may find it very difficult to tell strong encryption from weak encryption.

Just because an encryption program is included as part of a well-known software package does not necessarily mean it will be effective. Conversely, encryption functions in some software packages may be billed as offering only moderate security while in fact they are very difficult to break, such as the encryption function in PKZip.

The Complete Guide to E-Security

We have already looked at PGP, a program I highly recommend. However, it is not the only freeware encryption program of value on the Internet. There are a few other programs I like and use as part of my total e-security planning. In this chapter I will briefly review these programs, as well as discuss passwords and encryption built into other software. Because these programs are freeware, I recommend that anyone interested in e-security download copies of each of these programs and incorporate them into their e-security and communications planning.

NORTON SECRET STUFF

A program from Symantec Corporation, the same people who make Norton Utilities, Norton Anti-Virus, et. al., Norton Secret Stuff (**ftp://ftp1.symantec.com/misc/nss.exe**) allows the creation of self-extracting encrypted files. The advantage of self-extracting files is that the recipient of the file need not possess the encryption program in order to extract and use the information. All that is necessary is for the recipient to know the password/passphrase originally used to encrypt the files. Norton Secret Stuff allows up to 2,000 files to be placed in any single encrypted archive. The program works well (as is to be expected from anything produced by Symantec Corporation), uses the strong Blowfish algorithm to encrypt files, and allows passwords consisting of any keyboard character ranging in length from 3 to 50 characters. Norton Secret Stuff runs under Windows 3.1/95/98/NT, and the self-extracting files can be recovered by any system that can handle DOS.

There is, however, one major disadvantage to Norton Secret Stuff—it uses only a 32-bit encryption key, making the encrypted files susceptible to basic cryptanalysis. You do not normally expect to find major weaknesses in Norton products, but the weakness is intentional in this case. U.S. law prohibits export of robust encryption, classifying strong encryption as munitions, thus requiring the Symantec Corporation to use a weak key in a pro-

Encryption Programs

gram it makes available for free on the Internet. As for the ability to break Norton Secret Stuff encryption, there is a program available on the Internet called No More Secret Stuff (NMSS), which is specifically designed to defeat Norton Secret Stuff. NMSS will in fact usually defeat Norton Secret Stuff but may take as many as 10 to 15 days to accomplish this.

Does susceptibility to cryptanalysis invalidate Norton Secret Stuff as a useful security program? The answer to that question depends much on your security requirements. If you have significant proprietary information that you need to protect from a determined competitor, 32-bit encryption simply isn't sufficient no matter what encryption algorithm/program you use. However, the ability to archive up to 2,000 files in a self-extracting format readable on any computer that can handle DOS and Norton's reputation for reliability make Norton Secret Stuff worth considering for moderate security needs.

SECURITY BOX

Security Box
(**http://www.msi-a.fr/eng/sboxf/sbox_freeware.htm**) is an encryption program developed and distributed by Methode et Solution Informatique S.A. in France. Security Box uses a 128-bit key with the Triple-DES algorithm to encrypt files.

Once Security Box is set up on your computer, it places an icon on your desktop called "Encode." To encrypt a file, simply drag it over the Encode icon. Security Box opens a confirmation window asking if you want to encrypt the file. Click on "Yes" and a window opens where you can enter a passphrase to be used to secure the file. Security Box also allows you to enter "Tips to Retrieve the Password," a line of text where you can enter some information to help you remember the password for the encrypted file. Obviously, any clues you give to your password weaken the security of the encrypted information, but there may be some application for this line of text. (There is nothing that says you MUST use this line to provide clues to the file's password.)

The Complete Guide to E-Security

Now, click on the "Encrypt" button and Security Box encrypts the chosen file, replacing the original file with the encrypted version. Security Box retains the original name of the file, appending a .BOX extension to it.

To decrypt a file encrypted with Security Box, just drag the encrypted file over the "Encode" icon on your desktop. Enter the password for the file and then click on the "Decrypt" button. Security Box decrypts the file and places it on your desktop.

It is interesting to note that the license agreement states that Security Box "employs encryption systems authorised by the French Service Central de la Sécurité des Systèmes d'Information (SCSSI - Central Service for Information Systems Security)." Now, even though Security Box uses 128-bit Triple-DES and *seems* to offer a very robust encryption, it pays to be suspicious. France has not generally been agreeable to private use of strong encryption, and there may be a back door or some other weakness in Security Box that would allow access to encrypted files by the French government.

ABI CODER

ABI Coder (**http://www.abisoft.net/Coder.exe**) uses both the 128-bit BlowFish and the 192-bit Triple-DES algorithms. ABI Coder allows encryption of both files and folders. Encrypted files can be sent easily as e-mail attachments allowing ABI Coder to be used as part of your online communications security. ABI Coder also allows you to create self-decrypting files so that you can send an ABI encrypted file to someone who does not have ABI Coder installed on his computer.

Concerning the algorithms, the ABI Coder help file states:

ABI- CODER 3.5 uses a 128 bit Blowfish algorithm as well as a 192 bit Triple-DES encryption algorithm for backwards compatibility with our previous versions.

Encryption Programs

Algorithm Descriptions:

Blowfish: Blowfish is a symmetric block cipher that can be used as a drop-in replacement for DES or IDEA. It takes a variable-length key, from 32 bits to 448 bits, making it ideal for both domestic and exportable use. Blowfish was designed in 1993 by Bruce Schneier as a fast, free alternative to existing encryption algorithms. Since then it has been analyzed considerably, and it is slowly gaining acceptance as a strong encryption algorithm. Blowfish is the primary encryption algorithm used by ABI- CODER 3.5.

Triple-DES: Triple-DES is a secure variation of the Data Encryption Standard first developed by IBM, and later in 1977 adopted by the U.S. Government.

The DES algorithm is still widely used and is still considered reasonably secure. There is no feasible way to break DES, however because DES is only a 64-bit (8 characters) block cipher, an exhaustive search of 2^{55} steps on average, can retrieve the key used in the encryption. Because of this it is common practice to protect data using Triple-DES.

Triple-DES is a 192 bit (24 characters) cipher that uses three separate 64 bit keys and encrypts data using the DES algorithm three times. ABI- CODER uses a variation that takes a single 192 bit (24 characters) key and then;
- encrypts data using first 64 bits (8 characters)
- decrypts same data using second 64 bits (8 characters)
- encrypts same data using the last 64 bits (8 characters)

Keys: While using the ABI- CODER it is important to enter keys at least 128 bits (16 characters) in length. While anything less then that can be considered reasonably secure only the 128 bit (16 characters) encryption can provide true security.

In order to ensure that you enter a key of sufficient length to allow maximum strength encryption, ABI Coder provides you with a key quality indicator. As you type in your key a small graph indicates the strength of your key from 1-bit to 192-bits.

ABI Coder is an excellent symmetric encryption program,

allowing incorporation of strong encryption into both file and e-mail security. One thing to remember when using ABI Coder to secure e-mail is that the ABI encrypted file must be sent as an attachment to your e-mail. Some users have attempted to copy and paste the encrypted data from ABI into the body of an e-mail message, however this does not work as it corrupts the file and cannot be decrypted by the recipient.

TWOFISH LITE—WITH KEY GENERATOR

Twofish Lite—with Key Generator (**http://members.xoom.com/evepaludan/twofish1.zip**) provides extremely secure encryption in a user-friendly package. The Twofish algorithm is the successor to the Blowfish algorithm and was one of the candidates to become the Advanced Encryption Standard for corporate, banking and government contract use in the United States. The well-known cryptologist and security expert Bruce Schneier developed Twofish Lite, as well as its predecessor Blowfish. Twofish Lite uses a 256-bit encryption key in the ECB (Electronic Code Book) mode, making cryptologic recovery of the key for all practical purposes an impossibility.

Use of Twofish Lite is extremely simple. Open the program and type in your key phrase (password) in the Key Phrase block. Press the "Generate Secure Key" button and Twofish Lite uses elliptic curves to generate a secure key from your key phrase, which will appear in the Secure Key block. Next press either the "Encrypt File" or "Decrypt File" button depending on what you want to do. This opens a "browse" window allowing you to choose the file you wish to use.

Once the file is chosen, Twofish Lite asks you to provide a name for the output file, and choose a location where it will be saved. By default Twofish Lite saves encrypted files with the .TWO extension, however you have the option of assigning any extension you wish to use. When decrypting a file you must provide the proper file extension. If you don't know the file's original format, Twofish Lite will save it without a file extension requiring use of a file viewer (such as Quick View) to determine the file format and choose an application to view the decrypted file.

Twofish Lite provides very secure encryption of individual files, and works well on multiple files archived by other programs, such as Zip files. In order to decrypt files encrypted with Twofish Lite, one must have the Twofish Lite with Key Generator program installed on his computer. Twofish Lite does not wipe the original (plaintext) file when it encrypts, so it is important to remember to destroy the plaintext file after encryption if using Twofish Lite to secure files on the same system where they are encrypted.

Twofish Lite comes with a detailed help manual, which explains the use of the program, as well as giving basic insight into general information security procedures.

IRON KEY

Iron Key (**http://inv.co.nz/download/ikey.exe**) is the freeware version of INV Softworks' Silver Key encryption program. Iron Key places an icon on your Windows Desktop, allowing you to simply drag any item you wish to encrypt over the icon. Iron Key then opens a dialog window asking you to enter a password for the file. After you have chosen your password, Iron Key uses the DES algorithm in ECB (Electronic Code Book) mode to encrypt the file and create a self-decrypting archive. Iron Key does not ask you to verify your password, so type carefully when you enter it. Your encrypted file is placed on the Windows Desktop and can be sent as an attachment to e-mail. Iron Key does not destroy the original file.

To decrypt an Iron Key encrypted file simply click on the file. Iron key opens a dialog window asking for the password for the file. Then Iron Key opens a second dialog window asking for you to select a target directory where your decrypted file will be placed. Because an Iron Key encrypted file is self-decrypting, you do not need to have Iron Key software installed on your computer to decrypt the file. This makes Iron key useful for sending information through e-mail to recipients with whom you have arranged a password for decryption in advance.

KRYPTEL LITE

Kryptel Lite (**http://inv.co.nz/download/krlite.exe**) is another program from INV Softworks; the freeware version of their excellent Kryptel encryption software. Kryptel Lite places an icon on your Windows Desktop on installation. When you encrypt a file with Kryptel Lite, simply drag the file you want to encrypt over the Kryptel Lite icon. Kryptel Lite opens a dialog box and asks for a pass-phrase. Once you enter your pass-phrase Kryptel Lite encrypts the file and deletes the original. The encrypted file is appended with the .edc suffix, and the icon changes to show a padlock on top of documents.

To decrypt a Kryptel Lite encrypted document, drag the document over the Kryptel Lite icon. This opens a dialog box asking for the required pass-phrase. After you enter the correct pass-phrase Krypte Lite restores the encrypted document to its original configuration. Kryptel Lite does not make a self-decrypting archive, so you must have Kryptel Lite software installed on your computer in order to encrypt or decrypt documents.

VGP ENCRYPTION EDITOR

VGP Encryption Editor (**http://www.parisien.org/down/vgp.zip**) works much like Notepad in Windows. However, with the VGP Encryption Editor you have the ability to encrypt any text written to it. You can thereafter cut and paste this encrypted text into an e-mail message or save the encrypted text as a file.

Encryption Programs

VGP Encryption Editor uses a multi-pass encryption function, with one of the passes using the strong Blowfish algorithm.

VGP Encryption Editor allows you to establish a "password pick list," which is a list of names with specific passwords associated with each name. The list sits in an encrypted file on your hard drive. When creating messages you may simply choose from the list the name of the individual to whom you are sending the message and VGP will encrypt the message with the associated password. This allows you to develop a complicated password that VGP remembers for you. It is important to remember however that this is symmetric encryption (using the same key to encrypt and decrypt). If you repeatedly use the same key this weakens your overall security. Furthermore, if your key is ever compromised, all messages encrypted with that key can be decrypted and read!

VGP Encryption Editor is a small program, allowing one to run it from a floppy disk. This is an advantage for someone who travels frequently or uses several different computers.

DIAMOND PC1 CIPHER-128 AND X-MESSAGE

Diamond PC1 Cipher-128 and X-Message (**http://www.diamondcs.com.au/products/cipher.zip**) (**http://www.diamondcs.com.au/products/xmessage.zip**) is a 128-bit freeware encryption program offered by Diamond Computer Systems. Designed to provide e-mail security, this program has a user-friendly interface. You may store passwords associated with a specific user/e-mail address, or enter a password each time you encrypt a message.

Concerning the security of the Diamond PC1 Cipher, the Readme file states:

This freeware utility allows you to encrypt text (email, text files, etc.) using PC1 128-bit encryption, generally for sending in an email. How secure is 128-bit encryption? 128-bit encryption allows for a pos-

The Complete Guide to E-Security

sible 340282366920938463463374607 43 keys (or 340 million million million million million million different keys). Although this level is regarded as extremely secure, encryption is only as strong as its password. A password such as "p*2%d^&cM:$1!;$/" would render cracking virtually impossible.

The Diamond Cipher program allows you to maintain passwords in a password manager, thereby allowing use of strong passwords stored within the program itself.

In addition to it's PC1 Cipher, Diamond Computer Systems offers a freeware encryption program called X-Message. X-Message creates password protected self-decrypting files. It allows passwords up to 16-characters in length, and encrypts text using a 128-bits key. To use X-Message simply type or paste your message into the block provided, enter a password in the password block, and click on the "Make It" button. X-Message creates a self-decrypting file called "message.exe" and stores it in the same directory as the X-Message program itself. To send your encrypted message, simply attach it as a file to any e-mail message.

The recipient of the file just double clicks the file, which opens a window with the message: "This X-Message has been password-locked. Please enter the password (case sensitive)." Enter the correct password and click "OK" and the message decrypts and is displayed in a window on your computer-screen. Of course, an incorrect password means the file does not decrypt.

My one concern with the Diamond PC1 Cipher and X-Message is that the encryption algorithm used in these programs is proprietary to Diamond Computer Systems, and has not been extensively tested. Still both are easy-to-use programs for sending encrypted text through e-mail, and may therefore be useful for some encryption needs. Further testing of the algorithm may confirm its strength, or indicate a hidden weakness.

SCRAMDISK

ScramDisk
(**http://www.scramdisk.clara.net**). One of the major complaints often raised about using encryption to secure files is that encryption is inconvenient. Every time one wants to use a secured file it must be decrypted, and then re-encrypted when finished. ScramDisk solves this problem by creating a "scrambled disk" on your computer. This is actually an encrypted partition on a selected drive. Once installed, it appears as just another drive in Windows. ScramDisk uses on-the-fly encryption/decryption to secure files stored on this drive and grant access to the files when they are needed.

When you set-up ScramDisk, it will first ask you to choose the disk size you want to create. This can be any size, up to the amount of free space you have available on your selected drive (up to 4 GB). You then choose an encryption algorithm to use for securing your files stored in the ScramDisk. The algorithms currently available in ScramDisk are Blowfish, TEA-16-pass, TEA-32-pass, IDEA, DES-56-bit, Square, and Misty.

After choosing your encryption algorithm you are asked to choose passwords to secure your ScramDisk. There are four separate password blocks. You are not forced to use all four blocks, but it improves your security by doing so. Another use for the four separate passwords is to require multiple authorities to access a secure drive. One could require up to four separate individuals to enter a password in order to access the ScramDisk partition. You may also choose to have ScramDisk display the password field in a red, TEMPEST defeating font.

ScramDisk then creates a scrambled disk (encrypted partition) and stores it's access in the area you designate. By default ScramDisk identifies your partition with the suffix .SVL. However, ScramDisk gives you the option of assigning an alias to your partition so that it appears with a .DLL, .RND, .ZIP, or

The Complete Guide to E-Security

.DAT suffix. For even greater security, ScramDisk gives you the option of hiding access to your partition in a .WAV or .BMP file (steganography).

ScramDisk also gives you the option of setting hot-key dismount for your ScramDisk partition, as well as having the partition dismount after a set amount of inactivity. I use both of these options, allowing me to secure all the personal information on my computer, and having it done automatically if I make the mistake of leaving my computer unattended with the ScramDisk partition mounted.

When your ScramDisk partition is mounted it appears just like another disk under Windows. You can instruct programs to save files to this "disk" (partition). You can create separate folders therein and drag and drop files into these folders. When your ScramDisk is un-mounted it encrypts everything stored in it with the algorithm you selected when setting up the partition, and disappears from the "My Computer" folder of Windows. You thus have a strongly encrypted, hidden partition on your computer where you can protect your secrets.

Finally, when you download your copy of ScramDisk, you get an extensive user manual that provides clear instruction for using ScramDisk and a well-written overview of computer security.

DPCRYPTO

DPCrypto

(**http://dpaehl.notrix.de**) is a multi-algorithm encryption engine designed by Dirk Paehl in Germany. Mr. Paehl defines DPCrypto as "mindware" as opposed to freeware. He asks that if you decide to keep DPCrypto for your use that you send him whatever you think the program is worth. DPCrypto is designed to encrypt files, although there is nothing to prevent you from sending encrypted files as attachments to e-mail thereby using DPCrypto for secure communications. Simply select a file you wish to encrypt, designate your output file, select your algorithm and enter a password, and then click on either the "Encrypt" or "Decrypt" button. DPCrypto allows you to select from the following encryption algorithms:

Blowfish	448-bit Key
Gost	256-bit Key
MARS	1248-bit Key
RC6	2048-bit Key
Rijndael	256-bit Key
Twofish	256-bit Key

DPCrypto does not overwrite the input, and creates as a default the output file using the input file name with the suffix DPc. The multiple encryption algorithms allowed by DPCrypto allows you to add an additional layer of security to your file encryption by varying the algorithms used to encrypt different files. If you attempt to decrypt a file using the wrong algorithm, DPCrypto informs you that you have entered an incorrect password. You cannot tell which algorithm was used to encrypt a file just by looking at the encrypted text. While all the algorithms used in DPCrypto are currently considered to be very strong, should a weakness ever be identified in any one of the algorithms, you would have the option of immediately switching to another algorithm.

> *"Continue steadfast, and with a proper sense of your dependence on God, nobly defend those rights which heaven gave and no man ought to take from us."*
> —Provincial Congress of Massachusetts, 1774

PASSWORD AND ENCRYPTION BUILT INTO OTHER SOFTWARE

Almost all home computer systems include some sort of word processing and spreadsheet software. One of the most popular word processors is Microsoft Word, which is often accompanied by Microsoft Excel. These Microsoft Office products come with a built-in password/encryption function. You can assign a password to prevent documents you create from being opened, or you may allow the documents to be opened and read, but require a password in order to modify or edit the document in question.

To use the Microsoft Office password function, simply create the document and then click on "Save As . . ." under the File Menu. In the "Save As . . . " window click on the "Options . . ." button. In the space provided enter a password you want to use to protect your document from being read or modified. Click OK, confirm your password, and your document is now password protected. In order to open or modify the document in question you will be required to enter the appropriate password.

As a security function these password options are not very effective. To be fair, security was not the primary concern of Microsoft when producing its Office products. The fact that Microsoft Office offers any security option at all is a point in its favor, and the password option will keep out the merely curious or those individuals who obtain inadvertent access to a protected document.

As the primary means of protecting your documents, however, the password option in Microsoft Office products should not be relied upon. There are password-cracking programs available that are specifically designed to recover these Microsoft passwords.

One of the leading companies dealing in password recovery is Access Data Corporation in Provo, Utah (**http://www.access-data.com**). Access Data sells password recovery programs that can break the password protection of MS Office and other products in just a few minutes. I have used Access Data Corporation password recovery programs as well as similar programs from other companies and find that these programs are VERY effective.

Simply put, if you need to ensure protection of information on your computer system, do not rely solely on the low-level

Encryption Programs

password function built into word processors and the like. To provide security for your system, use products specifically designed for security. You wouldn't use a security program to write a well-formatted document, so don't use a word processor to secure that document!

". . . Whenever any form of government becomes destructive to these ends it is the right of the people to alter or abolish it . . ."
—American Declaration of Independence

STEGANOGRAPHY

Steganography is derived from the Greek *steganos*, meaning covered or secret, and *-graphy*, meaning writing. Over the centuries there have been several methods of hiding messages. Every schoolboy knows the story of Histiaeus, who was held prisoner during the 5th century B.C. by King Darius in Susa. Now, Histiaeus needed to send a secret message to his son-in-law Aristagoras in the city of Miletus. Histiaeus shaved the head of a slave and tattooed the message on his scalp. When the slave's hair had grown long enough to conceal the message, Histiaeus dispatched him to Aristagoras. This method worked for Histiaeus, but it is not very practical today.

In his book *Codes, Ciphers, and Secret Languages* Fred B. Wrixon relates a story about Sir John Trevanion that gives a fine historical example of steganography. About 1660, Trevanion, a Royalist, was captured by the Puritans and imprisoned in Colchester Castle on the southeast coast of England. While in prison, Sir John received the following letter:

Worthie Sir John:
Hope, that is ye beste comfort of ye afflicted, cannot much, I fear help me, help you now. That I would say to you, is this only: if ever I may be able to requite that I do owe you, stand not upon asking me. 'Tis not much that I can do: but what I can do, bee ye verie sure I

wille. I knowe that, if dethe comes, if ordinary men far it, it frights not you, accounting it for a high honour, to have such a rewarde of your loyalty. Pray yet that you may be spared this soe bitter, cup. I fear not that you will grudge any sufferings; only if bie submission you can turn them away, 'tis the part of a wise man. Tell me, an if you can, to do for you anythinge that you wolde have done. The general goes back on Wednesday. Restinge your servant to command.

—R.T.

This letter may be somewhat difficult for us to follow today, but it apparently aroused no suspicions among Sir John's jailers, as it was delivered to him in due course. After reading the message, Sir John asked for an hour to pray alone in the castle's chapel—not an unusual request considering the fate of those imprisoned in Colchester Castle—because he had noted something in the letter his jailers had not: the third letter following each punctuation mark of this letter spelled out a brief message: *panel at east end of chapel slides.*

Although there have been several methods of steganography throughout history, for our purposes we will discuss computer-based programs that allow us to hide text messages in pictures and sound files.

In any computer program there is space that is not actually used by the program itself—space that could be filled with something else (such as a hidden message). Steganography looks for the least significant bit in the various graphic and sound files and replaces that bit with a portion of the message to be hidden. The human eye and ear is not significantly sensitive to detect this minor change, and thus there is generally no visually or audibly detectable change to the file in which a message is being hidden. There is, however, the possibility of determining the file size of a known graphic file and comparing it to a like graphic suspected of carrying a hidden message. A file with a hidden message will always be larger than a file without the extra text hidden in its structure.

Encryption Programs

So, just why would anyone want to hide messages in pictures or other files? The most likely reason is to disguise the existence of the message itself. There are countries that suppress the rights of their citizens to freely express their views, and human rights abuses are seldom reported in the government-controlled press. Even in a relatively free and open society such as the United States, there are viewpoints that cannot be openly expressed.

Once you have decided to use steganography to send private messages you will need to develop a safe method of doing so. Simply sending graphics or sound files back and forth between individuals is not very effective. Retransmitting the same picture will certainly raise the suspicion of anyone who may be paying attention. You may be able to send different graphics or sound files back and forth under some pretext, but this, too, can attract attention after a while. Furthermore, sending files directly from your account to the account of another person establishes a direct link between the two of you, even if the true content of your messages is never discovered. Using remailers to send steganography is not an option, since most remailers don't handle attachments that well, if at all.

One effective way to use steganography is by posting graphics containing hidden messages to a Web page. Create a Web page, the content of which will draw little attention. The content should lend itself to the posting of graphics or sound files. You may simply want to design a Web page that is a collection of different graphics and sound files. Messages are passed by using steganography to hide them in selected files posted to the Web page. Anyone knowing which file contains the hidden message simply copies it from the Web page (right click with your mouse and Save As). Once the file is copied, use the appropriate steganography program and password to recover the message.

There are several steganography programs available to those of us interested in using hidden writing. Some of these are:

Contraband Hell Edition—This steganography program hides text in .BMP files. Contraband Hell Edition offers strong encryption.

Hide and Seek—Using the strong Blowfish encryption algorithm, Hide and Seek hides text in both .GIF and .BMP files. It also offers a file-wiping option ensuring secure deletion of programs from your computer.

In The Picture—This is a Windows-95 based program that hides text in .BMP files. In The Picture offers multiple encryption keys and a drag-and-drop feature, making it easy to use.

JSteg and JSteg Shell—JSteg is the one steganography program that lets you hide text in .JPG format images. Using JSteg Shell in the Windows 95/98/NT environment is easy and offers 40-bit encryption to increase the security of your files.

S-Tools—This is my favorite steganography program. The current version, S-Tools 4, allows you to hide text in .BMP, .GIF, and .WAV files. S-Tools 4 offers a drag-and-drop feature and various encryption algorithms to secure your messages. The previous version of S-Tools (Version 3) is also an excellent program but lacks the drag-and-drop feature of Version 4. The only complaint I have with S-Tools is that the two versions are not compatible (files hidden with Version 3 cannot be recovered with Version 4). S-Tools is offered as freeware, which is just one more point in favor of this excellent program.

Snow—Snow allows you to hide text files in text files!

There are various other steganography programs available, but this list should give you a basic starting point. One place to find steganography programs and information on the Internet is **http://members.tripod.com/steganography/stego.html**, but you can find many other sources by using a search engine to search the word "steganography."

Chapter 9

Securely Deleting or Hiding Files

"The only freedom which deserves the name is that of pursuing our own good, in our own way, so long as we do not attempt to deprive others of theirs, or impede their efforts to obtain it."
— John Stuart Mill

If you have been careful to follow the e-security techniques taught in this book you have a very secure communications protocol in place. There is, however, one other aspect that must not be overlooked, and that is properly deleting messages and files you no longer want.

Simply dragging a file or folder to the "trash bin" on your desktop or using the "delete" function from the menu does not completely get rid of the file or folder. Obviously, anything dragged into the trash bin can be dragged out again until the trash is emptied. The delete function only removes the file or folder name from the directory and marks the space it occupies on the disk as now being usable to store other programs, files, and folders. Using a disk management tool (such as Norton Utilities), it is a simple matter to recover the complete content of a deleted document. Norton Utilities "Unerase Wizard" makes this a very simple process indeed. Even if the document you are

The Complete Guide to E-Security

trying to recover has been partially overwritten, it is still possible to recover portions of the document using Norton Disk Edit or other system management and data recovery tools.

SECURE DELETE

To completely remove a file or folder from your system you must use a secure delete function. If you have PGP installed on your computer (and you do if you have been paying attention) you already have a secure delete function available. Simply choose the file or folder you want to securely delete and click on that file or folder with your right mouse button. Now choose PGP and Wipe. PGP will then securely delete the file or folder, completely wiping it from your system. It cannot be recovered!

You should make a habit of using PGP Wipe or some other secure delete program to remove unwanted files and folders from your system.

Additionally, it is important to ensure that all free space on your system is kept clear of residual data. Free space is that space on the disk that is not currently occupied by a program or file of some type. As we have seen previously, unless you use a secure delete function, when you delete a file the data remains on the disk and the space the file occupied is marked as free space. Over the course of time, the free space on your disk can be left with quite a bit of accessible data. To be sure that this data is not recoverable, you should defragment your hard drive frequently and wipe the free space off the disk to remove any residual data. Commercial programs (such as Norton Utilities) have functions to wipe the free space on your disks, and there are various freeware/shareware programs available online to do the same thing.

One program I have found useful for securely deleting files is SecureTrayUtil, designed by Sarah Dean, a software developer in Longwood, Florida. Dean's SecureTrayUtil allows for hotkey shredding of sensitive files and allows you to set up a self-destruct function to destroy targeted files on your system.

Securely Deleting or Hiding Files

Hotkey shredding destroys selected files when a particular combination of keys is pressed. For example, if you are a bookie and you maintain a record of bets taken in a particular file on your computer, you can set a hotkey, or combination of keys (e.g., Cntl-Shift-F6), which, when pressed, causes the utility to secure erase/shred that file. Comes in handy if you are sitting at your computer when the guys with the black hoods and MP5 submachine guns kick in the front door and seize your computer!

SecureTrayUtil is available on Dean's Web site: **http://www.fortunecity.com/skyscraper/true/882/**. Additionally, she has posted an excellent review of the various secure delete programs currently available online and makes some useful observations concerning these programs.

After reviewing the various secure delete programs available, choose the one that best meets your personal needs. The issue here is simply to be sure to use a secure delete program to prevent your sensitive files from being recovered once you have deleted them!

HIDING FILES

"Just because you're paranoid doesn't mean they're not out to get you."

There are several things you may do to keep your sensitive computer files from being found. As with the principle of steganography, if your files are not found by those who would compromise them, they can't be compromised.

Camouflage

There is an old saying, "to hide a tree, place it in the forest." This can also apply to hiding your computer files. The first thing we may do to hide a file is to simply place it among several other files that would be of no real interest to someone looking

The Complete Guide to E-Security

for sensitive information on our computer system. As an example, I have several hundred 3.5-inch floppy disks and a fair number of 100 MB zip disks, all containing various files and programs. Among these many disks are also disks promoting various Internet services and other free disks obtained from computer and game magazines. A text file, or even several text files saved on one of these disks, could contain sensitive information and simply be lost among the mass of other files. Of course, you would want this file named something innocuous. A file named "WAR PLANS" is sure to attract attention, but one more "Read" file may be overlooked by someone scanning directory listings for items of interest. Of course given time, every file listed in each directory could be reviewed, but this might require more time than the opposition is willing to expend.

Hidden Directory Listings

We can take our file-hiding one step further by making sure that our sensitive files are not in the normal directory listing. Changing the attribute of a file to "hidden" means it won't appear in the directory listing under DOS using the "dir" command, under Windows when looking at a disk/folder with "Windows Explorer," or under "My Computer." To change the attribute of a file to "hidden" under Windows, right-click on the file with your mouse and go to the "Properties" menu. Then simply mark the "hidden" box under attributes. The next time you look at the directory listing of your disk or folder, the hidden file will not be visible—after all, it's hidden. You can accomplish the same thing from DOS using the "attrib +h" command. The default on most systems is to not show hidden files, but this can be changed easily. Under DOS, simply place a comma after the directory command (dir,) to list all files and it will include hidden files. You will use one of these methods when you want to view the files you have hidden. The only advantage of using the "hidden" attribute is that it keeps files out of the directory listing. Still, it adds one more layer of security and should not be overlooked.

Securely Deleting or Hiding Files

Hidden Directories

Another option for hiding your files is to create a directory (folder) that is not accessible through Windows. This is done by creating a directory with extended ASCII characters using the "ALT" key. Although it is possible to use any of the extended ASCII characters in creating the directory, we will use "ALT255" to create a directory using a blank character. For purposes of this demonstration we will create this directory on a floppy disk, but there is nothing to prevent the same thing from being done on other drives.

Access your DOS prompt and place a floppy disk in your A: drive. From the DOS prompt access your A: drive and type the following:

md ALT255   (Hold down the ALT key and type the numbers 255)

This creates a directory on the A: drive where the directory name is a blank space.

Now change drives to your C: drive and copy files you want to protect to this directory by typing the following:

copy filename.txt a:\ALT255

This copies files into the ALT255 directory.

Finally, hide the ALT255 directory by using the attrib command as follows:

attrib +h ALT255

The directory is now hidden. If you view hidden files from within Windows you will be able to see the folder as with other hidden files, but Windows does not recognize the extended ASCII character in the directory name and will not allow you to access, move, or delete the folder. Someone attempting to access

The Complete Guide to E-Security

this folder through Windows will be unable to do so and may believe the disk is simply corrupted. This, like other tricks to hide files, can be easily defeated by anyone who understands how file structure works, but it will take time to find and access these hidden files.

Using the hidden attribute will keep someone from finding your sensitive files by quickly scanning your directory listings. The use of the ALT255 directory prevents the directory from being accessed from within Windows. Deleting a file and using a disk utility to recover it when needed makes it a bit more difficult to locate your hidden files, but each of these techniques is easily defeated by someone with unrestricted access to your computer and disks and a bit of time to work on finding the information in question. Because you are using PGP, anything someone discovers on your system will be encrypted, and thus unreadable, but the seizure of your files may result in their loss or destruction.

You, of course, have backup copies of all your sensitive files, but if every computer, drive, and disk in your home is destroyed or seized, what then? You can store backup copies of your files with a trusted friend or family member, but if all your files have just been seized, do you *want* to get to them? Perhaps not, depending on what caused the loss of your files in the first place! There is, however, a way to store your files off site and still be able to access them whenever needed. You can store your files out in cyberspace!

Hiding Files Online

There are several free Web-based e-mail services (Hotmail, Net@ddress, etc.) that allow users 3 to 5 megabytes of online storage space. Most of them even allow users to set up a system of folders for filing and sorting mail. Why not use these services to maintain an online file storage system?

To hide your files online, first create a Web-based e-mail account. Use one of the major services (such as Hotmail) to

Securely Deleting or Hiding Files

ensure that it will still be in business when you want to retrieve your files. Next use PGP conventional encryption to encrypt the files you want to store online.

It is important that you use conventional encryption in this case rather than using your public key, because if all copies of your PGP private key are lost or destroyed, the corresponding public key will be worthless. Since PGP conventional encryption uses symmetric encryption, you need only remember the passphrase used to encrypt the files and obtain a new copy of PGP in order to access them.

Finally, transmit the encrypted files to the account you have established as your online file system. You can then access the account and move the encrypted files to whatever folders you have established for your filing system.

Now, even if your computer is destroyed and all of your backup disks seized, you will still be able to recover your files from your file system hidden online. Once you have access to a new computer system, your first step is to download a new copy of PGP and set it up on your new system. Log in to your Web-based e-mail file system and copy the PGP-encrypted files to your new system. Enter the passphrase used to encrypt the files with PGP conventional encryption, and you have your information back.

One final note when using this online filing method: pay attention to how long your e-mail account may remain dormant before it is deleted. In many cases this is around 90 to 180 days (three to six months). The last thing you want to do is find your account deleted because you haven't accessed it in the past year. And you must be sure to use very strong password construction when encrypting your files before you store them online. Remember, the only thing protecting these files is the encryption used. If someone hacks into your account and copies your stored files, they can work on breaking the passphrase forever. Just be sure you use a passphrase that will take them forever to break!

Chapter 10

Communications Planning

> *SHB JIL BLL HRM QZH QYW EUX IZH BVC NIY USD WEC WXX*

It is important to build redundancy into your communications. So, when planning your communications, remember the acronym PACE: Primary, Alternate, Contingency, and Emergency.

If you rely on only one channel of communication you are effectively cut off from the world when that channel fails. But with PACE, you have several ways to turn.

Here is an example of PACE communications planning:

- Primary Communications Channel: PGP-encrypted e-mail is sent from your primary e-mail account and maintained and accessed from your home computer.

- Alternate Communications Channel: PGP-encrypted e-mail is sent from your secondary e-mail account and maintained and accessed from your work computer.

- Contingency Communications Channel: E-mail is sent from your Web-based HushMail account to another HushMail account, thereby taking advantage of the service's encryption function.

- Emergency Communications Channel: One-time pad encrypted message is read over the telephone and recorded on an answering machine that is checked at least daily.

Your primary and alternate communication channels are used pretty much interchangeably. You send and receive the majority of your online communication from home, but it is perhaps not unusual for you to send and receive personal e-mail from your business e-mail account. You maintain PGP on both your home and work computers and simply use the computer and e-mail account that is most convenient.

Your contingency communications channel is used for those occasions when you do not have access to your primary or alternate accounts but still need to send and receive messages. This might occur when you are away on a trip and don't have access to either your home or work computers and do not have PGP and your PGP key rings available. You can still get access to e-mail through public libraries, cybercafés, and such, and simply use a system that is prepared for this contingency.

Your emergency communication channel is used when all other communication channels fail, and when circumstances preclude waiting for these channels to be restored. As an example, you may employ your emergency communications channel when you have an important message to send but a storm has disabled the local telephone service, preventing you from accessing your e-mail accounts or the Internet to use a Web-based e-mail account. You may find that even with the regular telephone system not working, the cellular telephone system is still functioning. A message may be encrypted using your one-time pad and recorded on an answering machine/voice mail system

Communications Planning

maintained in another location not affected by the local telephone outage. These messages may even be received remotely by dialing in from another location and knowing the access code to retrieve the stored messages.

You must also look at possible threats to your communications and employ appropriate e-security to counter those threats. We all face a general threat from online criminals seeking to obtain our personal information for illegal acts, pornographers targeting our children online, and various government agencies that have forgotten that we, the people, have certain inalienable rights. However, your personal situation may result in additional threats being directed against you.

Do you conduct business online? If so, do you have competitors that would benefit from intercepting your e-mail or reading files stored on your computers? Have you gone through a divorce or been involved in another family dispute where people who know you well now seek to do you harm? Have you been involved in a dispute at work? Is there anyone who might, for whatever reason, want to do you harm or cause a little mischief? Even if none of these scenarios apply now, are you sure they never will?

By using e-security now you lessen the possibility of your privacy rights being compromised at some time in the future. Once you come to understand the importance of e-security there are several steps that you can take to begin improving your individual security posture:

Download and install a copy of PGP. Be sure to get a copy that contains both the Diffie-Hellman algorithm and the RSA algorithm to give you the greatest versatility in your communications. Encourage everyone with whom you communicate via e-mail to do the same.

Once you have PGP installed on your computer, record a copy of your PGP public key fingerprint and post your public key to one or more PGP Key Servers.

Establish e-mail accounts on one or more of the secure Web-based e-mail systems such as HushMail or ZipLip.

The Complete Guide to E-Security

Establish e-mail accounts on one or more of the standard Web-based e-mail systems, such as Hotmail or Yahoo! Mail. Establish these accounts from a public access computer, such as those in a public library or cybercafé, to prevent any association with your IP address.

Get a copy of the current remailer list. Practice sending anonymous mail until you can do it from memory. Send encrypted e-mail frequently through remailers, to include "Null mail" to help foil traffic pattern analysis. (Null mail is mail sent using the null: command in remailers. It tells the remailer to ignore and discard the message it has just received. The advantage of sending null mail is that you do not show a marked increase in the amount of e-mail you send as the result of any particular situation. For example, if you determine that you send an average of six pieces of e-mail daily, start sending four additional pieces of null mail. This gives you a baseline of 10. Now every day send exactly 10 pieces of e-mail. If tomorrow you have 9 pieces of real e-mail to send, then send only one piece of null mail. If the day after you only have two pieces of real e-mail to send, then send eight null e-mails. Thus, anyone attempting to conduct pattern analysis on the amount of e-mail you send has nothing to analyze: you always send 10 pieces of e-mail daily.

Create one-time pads and establish conventional encryption passwords. Provide these things to individuals with whom you will need to maintain secure communication. DO NOT send this information electronically. Provide it in person, or perhaps in a secure package sent by registered postal mail.

Make it a habit to stay apprised of advances and new products that can improve e-security. Security should be a consideration in all that you do, and this is especially true in the electronic environment!

Chapter 11

Online Communications and the Law

> "Mary had a crypto key, she kept it in escrow, and everything that Mary said the Feds were sure to know."
>
> —Sam Simpson

In the 1970s, Congress formed the Privacy Protection Study Commission to look at privacy issues as they related to American citizens. After a two-year study the commission concluded that a wide range of new laws and regulations were required to protect our privacy rights and freedoms. Unfortunately, Congress has generally ignored the recommendations of the commission, and very few have been made law. However, from time to time we see laws enacted that serve to protect our privacy rights and freedoms.

In 1986 Congress updated the Electronic Communications Privacy Act (ECPA) to prohibit the interception of stored and transmitted electronic messages, including e-mail. The ECPA was originally enacted in 1968 to protect us against telephone wiretapping. However, until the 1986 update (18 U.S.C. Sec. 2701-2711) there was no real protection for e-mail and similar online

The Complete Guide to E-Security

communications. While the ECPA provides basic guidelines for online privacy, these privacy rights may be abrogated as part of your contract/services agreement with the ISP. Still, the ECPA is a step in the right direction and should be read by those of us interested in protecting our online privacy. The 1986 update to the ECPA may be read in Appendix III of this book.

There are two sections of the ECPA to which I wish to draw your attention. First is the prohibition against accessing electronic communications without proper authorization:

Section 2701
"Offense. - Except as provided in subsection (c) of this section whoever –
(1) intentionally accesses without authorization a facility through which an electronic communication service is provided; or
(2) intentionally exceeds an authorization to access that facility; and thereby obtains, alters, or prevents authorized access to a wire or electronic communication while it is in electronic storage in such system shall be punished as provided in subsection (b) of this section."

The second is the section that prohibits disclosure of information contained within systems used for electronic communication:
Section 2702
"(a) Prohibitions. - Except as provided in subsection (b) –
(1) a person or entity providing an electronic communication service to the public shall not knowingly divulge to any person or entity the contents of a communication while in electronic storage by that service; and
(2) a person or entity providing remote computing service to the public shall not knowingly divulge to any person or entity the contents of any communication which is carried or maintained on that service -
(A) on behalf of, and received by means of electronic transmission from (or created by means of computer processing of communications received by means of electronic transmission from), a subscriber or customer of such service; and

Online Communications and the Law

(B) solely for the purpose of providing storage or computer processing services to such subscriber or customer, if the provider is not authorized to access the contents of any such communications for purposes of providing any services other than storage or computer processing."

As you can see, the law proscribes the unauthorized access and disclosure of electronic communications. Thus, you might assume that under the law your online communications are protected. Generally, this is true. However, there are exceptions provided under the law and, of course, systems operators and their ISP support personnel may disclose information that should be protected.

As an example of unauthorized disclosure and its resulting harm, we can look at the case of Timothy R. McVeigh and AOL. McVeigh was a Navy Senior Chief (not the guy who supposedly bombed the federal building in Oklahoma City) who maintained a personal account with AOL. On AOL you may publish a user profile where you can reveal certain information about yourself, which allows others to read these profiles and contact people with like interests. McVeigh created a user profile which, while not specifically stating that he was a homosexual, lead the navy to believe this to be the case. According to sworn testimony from the navy, in late 1997, personnel investigating the matter and attempting to identify the true identity of the owner of the profile simply called AOL and asked for the identity of the person owning the account with which the profile was associated. Apparently the naval personnel did not even identify themselves as representing the navy. They simply stated they were in receipt of a fax from that account and wanted to confirm the true identity of its owner. AOL identified the owner of the account as McVeigh and his state of residence as Hawaii. After obtaining this information from AOL, the navy brought charges against McVeigh and began the process to remove him from service.

Now, if McVeigh was involved in some sexual perversion and advertised this on the Internet, the navy was well justified in

The Complete Guide to E-Security

processing him out of military service. However, McVeigh's morality and judgment are not in question here; rather, I use this case to point out that even when the law and the policy of an ISP prohibit disclosure of personal information there is no guarantee that your account details will remain private.

In the case of *Steve Jackson Games v. United States* we see a federal court ruling that unread e-mail on the company computers of Steve Jackson Games was entitled to lesser protection under the ECPA. Steve Jackson Games was a company making various online role-playing games. It established a computer bulletin board to advertise its games and provide customer service. The bulletin board also provided for the exchange of information between users of the system. While in pursuit of a group of computer hackers known as "Legion of Doom," federal agents came to believe that one of these hackers was employed by Steve Jackson Games. In March 1990, with only an unsigned photocopy of a warrant, federal agents raided Steve Jackson Games and seized the online system and various other unrelated computer equipment. Even though neither Steve Jackson Games nor any other person was ever criminally charged as a result of the raid, federal agents refused to return the computer equipment for several months, resulting in significant loss to the business. Steve Jackson Games sued under the provisions of the Privacy Protection Act and the Electronic Communications Privacy Act and recovered damages.

It is important to note here that if you had been one of the individuals using the Steve Jackson Games online system to exchange messages, any of your messages that were on the system when it was seized are now part of the investigative records of federal law enforcement! *(Therefore, encrypt all online communications!!!)*

There are other laws that are designed to protect our electronically stored files. One example of this is found in the Privacy Protection Act, passed by Congress in 1980 and found in 42 U.S.C. Section 2000aa. This law reads as follows:

"Notwithstanding any other law, it shall be unlawful for a government officer or employee, in connection with the investigation or prosecution of a criminal offense, to search for or seize any work product materials possessed by a person reasonably believed to have a purpose to disseminate to the public a newspaper, book, broadcast, or other similar form of public communication . . ."

The intent of 42 U.S.C. Section 2000aa is to protect authors, reporters, and others preparing manuscripts for public release from having their work products seized during the course of an investigation. There are exceptions to this law, the most significant being that the work product of an author may be seized when it is believed that he is involved in the crime being investigated.

There are many older court decisions that may be of interest to the online privacy seeker. In *Katz v. United States* (1967), the court held that the right of privacy extends beyond mere tangible items and also includes "individual communications, personality, politics, and thoughts." In *NAACP v. Alabama* (1958), the court held that individuals have the right to maintain private associations, recognizing the "right of members to pursue their lawful private interest privately and to associate freely with others . . . without the deterrent effect which disclosure of membership lists is likely to have."

The thing to recognize about the law, e-security, and online privacy is that it simply isn't clear at this time. The law may offer some protection and may allow recovery of damages following the invasion of your privacy, but once your freedoms are trampled underfoot it may be impossible to recover them completely.

Pay attention to laws regarding your privacy rights, vote for laws that enhance or protect your privacy rights and freedoms, and support those elected representatives who work to protect your rights and freedoms, but remember that you are the best assurance of your own security.

The Complete Guide to E-Security

> *"The world isn't run by weapons anymore, or energy, or money. It's run by ones and zeros—little bits of data—it's all about electrons . . . There's a war out there, a world war. It's not about who has the most bullets; it's about who controls the information—what we see and what we hear, how we work, and what we think. It's all about information."*
> —Cosmo in the movie *Sneakers* (1992)

PRIVACY IN THE E-WORLD AND THE PHYSICAL WORLD

In my book *Privacy for Sale* I discussed, in detail, privacy in the physical world, touching only briefly on cyberspace and e-security. In this book I believe that it is important to touch briefly on things you can do in the physical world to enhance your e-security.

Someone wanting access to your online accounts, e-mail, and electronic files will have significant difficulty obtaining that access if you employ good e-security. If the desire to obtain access is strong enough, however, you may find that such snoops will target you in the physical world in order to obtain information about you to use in cracking your electronic accounts, e-mail, and files. Additionally, some criminals (and others) will gather information about people as a matter of course to use when the opportunity presents itself.

It is essential that you develop a general security consciousness in all that you do if you want to protect your security, privacy, and personal freedoms. The following recommendations are offered as general guidelines and should be used by everyone as a matter of course.

Guard your personal information, and do not use bits of information from your private life as keys to access your files or accounts. As an example, your bank and many credit card companies will ask for your mother's maiden name to use as a key in identifying you should you call with questions or instructions regarding your accounts. We also see this type of thing being

Online Communications and the Law

asked when you establish online accounts as a key in case you forget your password. Don't actually use your mother's maiden name as any type of security key or cross-check. After all, it's on your birth certificate and that's a public record.

Never, never, never give out your Social Security number unless specifically required to do so by law! The use of Social Security numbers as universal identifiers is an extremely dangerous precedent. Just Say No! With your Social Security number being the key to multiple accounts, failure of security in one account results in the compromise of all. (For details on this, read *Privacy for Sale*.)

Be aware of what you throw into the trash. Don't discard personal information (credit card statements, personal letters, bills, invoices, etc.) in a readable format. Buy and use a paper shredder, burn this information in your fireplace, or, as a minimum precaution, tear these documents into pieces and discard the pieces in separate trash cans.

Never reply to requests for information about your computer system, account log-in, or passwords. Don't put this type of information in user profiles, and never discuss this information over the telephone. If someone calls you on the telephone or sends you an e-mail and asks for information about your online accounts, e-mail, etc., there is a +99-percent chance this is someone attempting to gain unauthorized access to your account information. System administrators simply don't require this information to do their jobs, so there is no reason for them to call and ask for it.

Your private life should remain private. Develop the mind-set that you will not disclose information about yourself or your family as a matter of course. Decide that you will live privately and peacefully, and take back your rights from those who would trample them underfoot!

Chapter 12

A Final Word

"All we ask is to be let alone."
—Jefferson Davis,
President of the Confederated States of America, 1861

After reading this book, some may feel that it is antigovernment. That is certainly not my intent, although I do believe that for the past several years many of our federal agencies have shown an increasing disregard for the rights and freedoms of the American people. Others may think this book teaches criminals how to protect themselves from valid law-enforcement investigations. A criminal may use the information contained herein for evil purposes, just as an honest man may use this information for noble purposes; it is for that honest man that I have written this book.

There was a time when I was perhaps one of the strongest supporters of federal law enforcement, believing that the FBI was truly our nation's premier law enforcement agency. However, after seeing the atrocities at Ruby Ridge, Idaho, and Waco, Texas, where people died at the hands of our federal law enforcement agents, followed quickly by cover-ups of the circumstances surrounding these deaths, I began to wonder about the integrity of these agencies.

When I read the proposals by the Justice Department to conduct covert action against American citizens in their homes and limit private use of robust encryption technology, I began to wonder just how great a need there was to monitor private communications for criminal activity. With the all the effort and emphasis directed toward limiting private encryption, you'd think our federal law enforcement agents must have an extensive need to use electronic surveillance to capture dangerous criminals and protect us from attack by terrorists. The fact is, however, according to FBI Director Louis Freeh, in 1998 there were only 1,329 orders signed by judges allowing lawful electronic surveillance. This is not 1,329 orders authorizing the FBI to conduct electronic surveillance, rather a total of only 1,329 orders nationwide for all federal, state, and local law enforcement agencies. With only 1,329 orders for lawful electronic surveillance authorized, just why do the Department of Justice and other federal agencies think they need the capability to freely and easily monitor the communications of millions of Americans in general? Once we open this Pandora's box, who knows what evils we may unleash on our rights and freedoms.

The point to all of this is that many of our federal agencies (and perhaps our state and local agencies) have lost all regard for the rights and freedoms of the people. These agencies have forgotten that they are the servants, not the masters, of the American people. It is a sad state of affairs, but we must all be aware that in seeking to protect our personal freedoms, we may have to protect ourselves against government agencies that have forgotten the principles on which this great republic was founded.

Writing in the case of *Olmstead v. United States* in 1928, Justice Louis Brandeis recognized that the right to be left alone is the most comprehensive of rights and the right most valued by civilized men. It is my belief in this right that inspires my

A Final Word

writings. We all have the right to live a life free from the interference of government and our fellow citizens. This is especially true concerning the security of our private papers and our private communications.

The Fourth Amendment to the Constitution of the United States guarantees the right of the people to be secure in their persons, houses, papers, and effects . . . Clearly this security extends to our personal and private communications and our electronically stored papers and files today. Advancing technology does not, and cannot, do away with the underlying principles of the republic and the inalienable rights of the people.

Unfortunately, there are those who believe that we should get used to a little less freedom, that we should give up just a few of our guaranteed liberties in the name of safety. God forbid it! Those who advocate a lessening of our rights and freedoms are seldom acting out of good faith, for no rational man could for one moment believe that chipping away at this country's foundation could have any but a harmful effect upon its people. Whenever you hear someone advocate infringement of our rights in the name of safety, remember the words of Benjamin Franklin: "Those who would give up essential liberty to purchase safety deserve neither liberty nor safety."

By using the techniques and resources in this book you will greatly enhance the security of your private communications and help to maintain essential liberties by slowing the encroachment of rogue authority, social directive, and onerous laws that weaken personal freedom.

Appendix I

FBI Statement on Encryption

Statement of Louis J. Freeh,
Director, Federal Bureau of Investigation
on July 25, 1996
Before the
Committee on Commerce, Science, and Transportation
United States Senate
Regarding
Impact of Encryption on Law Enforcement and Public Safety

Thank you Mr. Chairman and members of the Committee for providing me with this opportunity to discuss with you an issue of extreme importance and of great concern to all of law enforcement, both domestically and abroad – the serious threat to public safety posed by the proliferation and use of robust encryption products that do not allow for timely law enforcement access and decryption.

First and foremost, the law enforcement community fully supports a balanced encryption policy that satisfies both the commercial needs of industry and law abiding individuals for robust encryption products while at the same time satisfying law enforcement's public safety needs. On the one hand, encryption is extremely beneficial when used legitimately to protect commercially sensitive information and communications. On the other, the potential use of such robust encryption products by a vast array of criminals and terrorists to conceal their criminal communications and information poses an extremely serious and, in my view, unacceptable threat to public safety. Recently, the President of the International Association of Chiefs of Police sent a letter to President Clinton expressing support for a balanced encryption policy that addresses the public safety concerns of law enforcement. Additionally, the National Sheriff's Association enacted a resolution last month also expressing their support for a balanced encryption policy and opposing any legislative efforts that would undercut the adoption of such a balanced policy.

The Complete Guide to E-Security

Since 1992, when AT&T announced its plan to sell a small, portable telephone device that would provide users with low-cost but robust voice encryption, public policy issues concerning encryption have increasingly has been debated in the United States. Since then, people concerned about privacy, commerce, computer security, law enforcement, national security, and public safety have participated in the dialogue regarding cryptography. On the international front, this past December, the multi-national Organization for Economic Cooperation and Development (OECD) meeting in Paris, France, convened an Experts Group to draft global cryptography principles, thus reflecting an increased global interest in and concern about the use and availability of encryption that can be used to endanger a nation's public safety and national security.

In addition, several Members of Congress have also joined this public discussion by introducing legislation which essentially would remove existing export controls on encryption and which would promote the widespread availability and use of any type of encryption product regardless of the impact on public safety and national security. However, the impact of these bills, should they be enacted, has not been lost on other Members of Congress as reflected in the letters to the sponsors of both Senate encryption bills by the Chairman and Vice-Chairman of the Senate Select Committee on Intelligence. Senators Specter and Kerrey indicated in their letters that they had concerns regarding these bills and expressed the opinion, which I fully endorse, that there is a "... need to balance U.S. economic competitiveness with the need to safeguard national security interests." To that balance, I would also add public safety and effective law enforcement.

Without question, the use of strong cryptography is important if the Global Information Infrastructure (GII) is to fulfill its promise. Data must be protected — both in transit and in storage—if the GII is to be used for personal communications, financial transactions, medical care, the development of new intellectual property, and a virtually limitless number of other applications. Our support for robust encryption stems from a commitment to protecting privacy and commerce.

But we are also mindful of our principal mission responsibilities: protecting America's public safety and national security in the myriad of criminal, terrorist, and espionage cases that confront us every day. Notwithstanding the accepted benefits of encryption, we have long

Appendix I

argued that the proliferation of unbreakable encryption—because of its ability to completely prevent our Nation's law enforcement agencies from understanding seized computer files and intercepted criminal communications which have been encrypted and then being able to promptly act to combat dangerous criminal, terrorist, and espionage activities as well as successfully prosecute them—would seriously and fundamentally threaten these critical and central public safety interests. The only acceptable answer that serves all of our societal interests is to foster the use of "socially-responsible" encryption products, products that provide robust encryption, but which also permit timely law enforcement and national security access and decryption pursuant to court order or as otherwise authorized by law.

Law enforcement is already beginning to encounter the harmful effects of conventional encryption in some of our most important investigations:

- In the Aldrich Ames spy case, where Ames was told by his Soviet handlers to encrypt computer file information to be passed to them.

- In a child pornography case, where one of the subjects used encryption in transmitting obscene and pornographic images of children over the Internet.

- In a major drug-trafficking case, where one of the subjects of one of the court-ordered wiretaps used a telephone encryption device which frustrated the surveillance.

- Some of the anti-Government Militia groups are now advocating the use of encryption as a means of preventing law enforcement from properly investigating them.

It is important to understand, as one can see from the cases I have cited, that conventional encryption not only can prevent electronic surveillance efforts, which in terms of numbers are conducted sparingly, but it also can prevent police officers on a daily basis from conducting basic searches and seizures of computers and files. Without an ability to promptly decrypt encrypted criminal or terrorist communications and

The Complete Guide to E-Security

computer files, we in the law enforcement community will not be able to effectively investigate or prosecute society's most dangerous felons or, importantly, save lives in kidnappings and in numerous other life and death cases. We simply will not be able to effectively fulfill our mission of protecting the American public.

In a very fundamental way, conventional encryption has the effect of upsetting the delicate legal balance of the Fourth Amendment, since when a judge issues a search warrant it will be of no practical value when this type of encryption is encountered. Constitutionally-effective search and seizure law assumes, and the American public fully expects, that with warrant in hand law enforcement officers will be able to quickly act upon seized materials to solve and prevent crimes, and that prosecutors will be able to put understandable evidence before a jury. Conventional encryption virtually destroys this centuries old legal principle.

There is now an emerging opinion throughout much of the world that there is only one solution to this national and international public safety threat posed by conventional encryption – that is, key escrow encryption. Key escrow encryption is not just the only solution; it is, in fact, a very good solution because it effectively balances fundamental societal concerns involving privacy, information security, electronic commerce, public safety, and national security. On the one hand, it permits very strong, unbreakable encryption algorithms to be used, which is essential for the growth of commerce over the GII and for privacy and information security domestically and internationally. On the other hand, it permits law enforcement and national security agencies to protect the American public from the tyranny of crime and terrorism. We believe, as do many others throughout the world, that technology should serve society, not rule it; and that technology should be designed to promote public safety, not defeat it. Key escrow encryption is that beneficial and balanced technological solution.

American manufacturers that employ encryption in their hardware and software products are undoubtedly the technology leaders in the world. American industry has the capability of meeting all of society's basic needs, including public safety and national security, and we, as responsible government leaders, should be sending a clear signal to industry encouraging them to do so. Key escrow encryption is "win-win" technology for societies worldwide. I know you agree that it

Appendix I

would be irresponsible for the United States, as the world's technology leader, to move towards the adoption of a national policy that would knowingly and consciously unleash on a widespread basis unbreakable, non-key escrow encryption products that put citizens in the U.S. and worldwide at risk.

Unfortunately, in recent months, the nearly exclusive focus of the public discussion concerning the encryption issue has been on its commercial aspects, particularly with regard to removing export controls. This narrow focus ignores the very real threat that conventional, non-key escrow encryption poses both domestically and internationally to public safety. We continue actively to seek industry's cooperation, assistance, and great expertise in producing key escrow encryption products as a critical part of an overall, balanced, and comprehensive encryption policy that would logically include an appropriate relaxation of export controls for key escrow products.

As for export controls, we have had ongoing discussions with industry, and industry has articulated the view that export controls needlessly hurt U.S. competitiveness overseas. But once again we need to carefully consider the facts and balance a number of competing interests. Although some strong encryption products can be found overseas, they are simply not ubiquitous, and, as of yet, they have not become embedded in the basic operating systems and applications found overseas.

Importantly, when the U.S. recently let it be known that it was considering allowing the export of encryption stronger than that now permitted, several of our close allies expressed strong concerns that we would be flooding the global market with unbreakable cryptography, increasing the likelihood of its use by criminal organizations and terrorists throughout Europe and the world, and thereby imperiling the public safety in their countries. Ironically, the relaxation of export controls in the U.S. may well lead to the imposition of import controls overseas. The international implications and likely reactions of foreign governments to the U.S. unilaterally lifting such export controls must be fully considered.

Given the fact that the use and availability of robust encryption is an issue of concern internationally, it is important to understand what steps other countries are taking to address these concerns. Recently, France, Russia and Israel have established domestic restrictions on the

The Complete Guide to E-Security

import, manufacturer, sale and use of encryption products, as not to endanger their public safety and national security. The European Union is moving towards the adoption of a key recovery-based key management infrastructure similar to that proposed for use within the United States. This plan, based upon the concept of using a "Trusted Third Party," allows for encryption keys to be escrowed with an independent but non-governmental party, thus allowing for lawful government access to such escrowed key pursuant to proper legal authority.

Lastly, we have heard the oft-repeated argument that the "genie is out of the bottle," and that attempts to influence the future use of cryptography are futile. This is simply not true; and we strongly disagree. If strong, key escrow encryption products proliferates both overseas and domestically which will not interoperate (at least in the long-term) with non-key escrow products, then escrowed encryption products will become the worldwide standard and will be used by almost everyone, including the criminal elements, in countries participating in the GII. It is worth noting that we have never contended that a key escrow regime, whether voluntarily or mandatorily implemented, would prevent all criminals from obtaining non-key escrowed encryption products. But even criminals need to communicate with others nationally and internationally, including not just their criminal confederates but also legitimate organizations such as banks. Accessible, key escrow encryption products clearly will be used by most if widely available, inexpensive, easy to use, and interoperable world-wide.

In closing, if one considers the broad range of public safety responsibilities that fall upon the law enforcement community, there is only one responsible course of action that we as government leaders must embark upon – to promote socially-responsible encryption products, products that contain robust cryptography but which also provide for timely law enforcement access and decryption – that is, key escrow encryption. The entire law enforcement community believes not only that the removal of export controls for encryption products that are non- law enforcement accessible is unwise, but that such an action would jeopardize our national security and the interests and safety of law-abiding citizens worldwide.

We look forward to working with you and your staff on this difficult issue and would be pleased to answer any questions you might have.

Appendix II

Online Security and Privacy Resources

The following organizations and businesses are those that I have found useful in developing e-security techniques and resources. Because of the ever-changing environment in cyberspace and the continual advances of technology, it is important to stay current in your understanding of e-security and privacy issues. The following list may assist you in this endeavor.

A listing here does not imply any specific association among the organizations, nor does a lack of listing mean that an organization or business does not have something of value to offer those of us seeking e-security and privacy online. It is simply not practical to attempt to list every resource one might find of value.

Finally, when dealing with any organization or business, you must make your own determination as to whether what is offered will meet your specific needs. I make no guarantees, except to say that I have personally found the following organizations, businesses, and Web sites interesting.

Center for Democracy and Technology
1634 Eye Street, NW, Suite 1100
Washington, D.C. 20006
Web site: **http://www.cdt.org**

Computer Professionals for Social Responsibility
P.O. Box 717
Palo Alto, CA 94302
E-mail: **webmaster@cpsr.org**
Web site: **http://www.cpsr.org**

Disappearing, Inc.
301 Howard Street, Suite 1920
San Francisco, CA 94105
E-mail: **info@disappearing.com**
Web site: **http://www.disappearing.com**

The Complete Guide to E-Security

Electronic Frontier Foundation
1550 Bryant Street, Suite 725
San Francisco, CA 94103-4832
E-mail: **ask@eff.org**
Web site: **http://www.eff.org**

Electronic Frontiers Georgia
4780 Ashford Dunwoody Road, Suite A-205
Atlanta, GA 30338
E-mail: **efga@efga.org**
Web site: **http://www.efga.org**

Electronic Privacy Information Center
1718 Connecticut Avenue, NW, Suite 200
Washington, D.C. 20009
E-mail: **info@epic.org**
Web site: **http://www.epic.org**

Network Associates, Inc.
3965 Freedom Circle
Santa Clara, CA 95054
Web site: **http://www.nai.com**

PrivacyX.Com Solutions, Inc.
541 Howe Street
Vancouver, British Columbia, Canada V6C 2C2
E-mail: **feedback@privacyx.com**
Web site: **http://www.privacyx.com**

ZDNet (Ziff-Davis)
650 Townsend Street
San Francisco, CA 94103
Web site: **http://www.zdnet.com**

Zero-Knowledge Systems, Inc.
888 de Maisonneuve East, 6th floor
Montreal, Quebec, Canada H2L 4S8
E-mail: **privacy@zeroknowledge.com**
Web site: **http://www.zeroknowledge.com**

Appendix II

The following is a list of e-security/privacy-related Web sites, some of which I use and enjoy and others that I have just recently discovered. They are listed here for your reference.

1on1 Mail	http://www.1on1mail.com
ASPPGP Remailer	http://www.itech.net.au/asptools/email.html
Counterpane	http://www.counterpane.com/labs/html
East Technologies	http://www.east-tec.com
First Cut	http://www.users.globalnet.co.uk/~firstcut/
Freedom Remailer	http://freedom.gmsociety.org/remailer/
IdZap	http://www.idzap.com
International PGP	http://www.pgpi.org
Jack B. Nymble	http://www.skuz.net/potatoware/jbn
John Doe	http://www.cix.co.uk/~net-services/jdo.htm
LokMail	http://mail.lokmail.net
Mail Anon	http://www.mailanon.com
The Nymserver	http://www.nymserver.com
Privacy Rights Clearinghouse	http://www.privacyrights.org
Private Idaho	http://www.eskimo.com/joelm/pi.html
Rivertown PGP Page	http://pgp.rivertown.com
Scramdisk	http://www.scramdisk.clara.net

The Complete Guide to E-Security

SecureNym   **http://www.securenym.net**

Somebody.Net   **http://www.somebody.net**

Ultimate Anonymity
http://www.ultimateanonymity/remailer.html

W3 – Anonymous Remailer
http://www.gilc.org/speech/anonymous/remailer.html

Websperts/Clandestination
http://www.websperts.net/home.shtml

It is also possible to download copies of security-related programs from the Internet. Some of these programs are in the public domain or are freeware, while most are shareware, asking a small registration fee if you decide to keep the program after evaluating it. One of the best places to download software from the Internet is from Simtel.Net (http://www.simtel.net/simtel.net/). Simtel.Net describes itself as a "worldwide distribution network for shareware, freeware, and public domain software." While visiting the Simtel.Net Web site, search its files using the key words "encryption," "security," and "password." This will give you numerous files to use to enhance your e-security.

Appendix III

Title 18 United States Code, Sections 2701-2711

ELECTRONIC COMMUNICATIONS PRIVACY ACT

Title 18 USC Sec. 2701. Unlawful access to stored communications

(a) Offense. - Except as provided in subsection (c) of this section whoever -
  (1) intentionally accesses without authorization a facility through which an electronic communication service is provided; or
  (2) intentionally exceeds an authorization to access that facility; and thereby obtains, alters, or prevents authorized access to a wire or electronic communication while it is in electronic storage in such system shall be punished as provided in subsection (b) of this section.
(b) Punishment. - The punishment for an offense under subsection (a) of this section is -
  (1) if the offense is committed for purposes of commercial advantage, malicious destruction or damage, or private commercial gain -
    (A) a fine under this title or imprisonment for not more than one year, or both, in the case of a first offense under this subparagraph; and
    (B) a fine under this title or imprisonment for not more than two years, or both, for any subsequent offense under this subparagraph; and
  (2) a fine under this title or imprisonment for not more than six months, or both, in any other case.
(c) Exceptions. - Subsection (a) of this section does not

apply with respect to conduct authorized -
(1) by the person or entity providing a wire or electronic communications service;
(2) by a user of that service with respect to a communication of or intended for that user; or
(3) in section 2703, 2704 or 2518 of this title.

Title 18 USC Sec. 2702. Disclosure of contents
(a) Prohibitions. - Except as provided in subsection (b) -
(1) a person or entity providing an electronic communication service to the public shall not knowingly divulge to any person or entity the contents of a communication while in electronic storage by that service; and
(2) a person or entity providing remote computing service to the public shall not knowingly divulge to any person or entity the contents of any communication which is carried or maintained on that service -
(A) on behalf of, and received by means of electronic transmission from (or created by means of computer processing of communications received by means of electronic transmission from), a subscriber or customer of such service; and
(B) solely for the purpose of providing storage or computer processing services to such subscriber or customer, if the provider is not authorized to access the contents of any such communications for purposes of providing any services other than storage or computer processing.
(b) Exceptions. - A person or entity may divulge the contents of a communication -
(1) to an addressee or intended recipient of such communication or an agent of such addressee or intended recipient; (2) as otherwise authorized in section 2517, 2511 (2)(a), or 2703 of this title;
(3) with the lawful consent of the originator or an addressee or intended recipient of such communication, or the subscriber in the case of remote computing service;

Appendix III

(4) to a person employed or authorized or whose facilities are used to forward such communication to its destination;
(5) as may be necessarily incident to the rendition of the service or to the protection of the rights or property of the provider of that service; or
(6) to a law enforcement agency -
   (A) if the contents -
      (i) were inadvertently obtained by the service provider; and
      (ii) appear to pertain to the commission of a crime; or
   (B) if required by section 227 of the Crime Control Act of 1990.

Title 18 USC Sec. 2703.
Requirements for governmental access

(a) Contents of Electronic Communications in Electronic Storage. - A governmental entity may require the disclosure by a provider of electronic communication service of the contents of an electronic communication, that is in electronic storage in an electronic communications system for one hundred and eighty days or less, only pursuant to a warrant issued under the Federal Rules of Criminal Procedure or equivalent State warrant. A governmental entity may require the disclosure by a provider of electronic communications services of the contents of an electronic communication that has been in electronic storage in an electronic communications system for more than one hundred and eighty days by the means available under subsection (b) of this section.

(b) Contents of Electronic Communications in a Remote Computing Service. - (1) A governmental entity may require a provider of remote computing service to disclose the contents of any electronic communication to which this paragraph is made applicable by paragraph (2) of this subsection -
   (A) without required notice to the subscriber or customer, if the governmental entity obtains a warrant issued under the Federal Rules of Criminal Procedure or equivalent State warrant; or

The Complete Guide to E-Security

(B) with prior notice from the governmental entity to the subscriber or customer if the governmental entity -
(i) uses an administrative subpoena authorized by a Federal or State statute or a Federal or State grand jury or trial subpoena; or
(ii) obtains a court order for such disclosure under subsection (d) of this section; except that delayed notice may be given pursuant to section 2705 of this title.
(2) Paragraph (1) is applicable with respect to any electronic communication that is held or maintained on that service -
(A) on behalf of, and received by means of electronic transmission from (or created by means of computer processing of communications received by means of electronic transmission from), a subscriber or customer of such remote computing service; and
(B) solely for the purpose of providing storage or computer processing services to such subscriber or customer, if the provider is not authorized to access the contents of any such communications for purposes of providing any services other than storage or computer processing.
(c) Records Concerning Electronic Communication Service or Remote Computing Service. - (1)(A) Except as provided in subparagraph (B), a provider of electronic communication service or remote computing service may disclose a record or other information pertaining to a subscriber to or customer of such service (not including the contents of communications covered by subsection (a) or (b) of this section) to any person other than a governmental entity.
(B) A provider of electronic communication service or remote computing service shall disclose a record or other information pertaining to a subscriber to or customer of such service (not including the contents of communications covered by subsection (a) or (b) of this section) to a governmental entity only when the governmental entity -
(i) obtains a warrant issued under the Federal Rules of Criminal Procedure or equivalent State warrant;
(ii) obtains a court order for such disclosure under subsection (d) of this section;

Appendix III

(iii) has the consent of the subscriber or customer to such disclosure; or

(iv) submits a formal written request relevant to a law enforcement investigation concerning telemarketing fraud for the name, address, and place of business of a subscriber or customer of such provider, which subscriber or customer is engaged in telemarketing (as such term is defined in section 2325 of this title).

(C) A provider of electronic communication service or remote computing service shall disclose to a governmental entity the name, address, local and long distance telephone toll billing records, telephone number or other subscriber number or identity, and length of service of a subscriber to or customer of such service and the types of services the subscriber or customer utilized, when the governmental entity uses an administrative subpoena authorized by a Federal or State statute or a Federal or State grand jury or trial subpoena or any means available under subparagraph (B).

(2) A governmental entity receiving records or information under this subsection is not required to provide notice to a subscriber or customer.

(d) Requirements for Court Order. - A court order for disclosure under subsection (b) or (c) may be issued by any court that is a court of competent jurisdiction described in section 3127 (2)(A) and shall issue only if the governmental entity offers specific and articulable facts showing that there are reasonable grounds to believe that the contents of a wire or electronic communication, or the records or other information sought, are relevant and material to an ongoing criminal investigation. In the case of a State governmental authority, such a court order shall not issue if prohibited by the law of such State. A court issuing an order pursuant to this section, on a motion made promptly by the service provider, may quash or modify such order, if the information or records requested are unusually voluminous in nature or compliance with such order otherwise would cause an undue burden on such provider.

(e) No Cause of Action Against a Provider Disclosing

Information Under This Chapter. - No cause of action shall lie in any court against any provider of wire or electronic communication service, its officers, employees, agents, or other specified persons for providing information, facilities, or assistance in accordance with the terms of a court order, warrant, subpoena, or certification under this chapter.
(f) Requirement To Preserve Evidence. -
   (1) In general. - A provider of wire or electronic communication services or a remote computing service, upon the request of a governmental entity, shall take all necessary steps to preserve records and other evidence in its possession pending the issuance of a court order or other process.
   (2) Period of retention. - Records referred to in paragraph (1) shall be retained for a period of 90 days, which shall be extended for an additional 90-day period upon a renewed request by the governmental entity.

Title 18 Sec. 2704. Backup preservation
(a) Backup Preservation. - (1) A governmental entity acting under section 2703(b)(2) may include in its subpoena or court order a requirement that the service provider to whom the request is directed create a backup copy of the contents of the electronic communications sought in order to preserve those communications. Without notifying the subscriber or customer of such subpoena or court order, such service provider shall create such backup copy as soon as practicable consistent with its regular business practices and shall confirm to the governmental entity that such backup copy has been made. Such backup copy shall be created within two business days after receipt by the service provider of the subpoena or court order.
   (2) Notice to the subscriber or customer shall be made by the governmental entity within three days after receipt of such confirmation, unless such notice is delayed pursuant to section 2705(a).
   (3) The service provider shall not destroy such backup copy until the later of -

Appendix III

(A) the delivery of the information; or

(B) the resolution of any proceedings (including appeals of any proceeding) concerning the government's subpoena or court order.

(4) The service provider shall release such backup copy to the requesting governmental entity no sooner than fourteen days after the governmental entity's notice to the subscriber or customer if such service provider -

(A) has not received notice from the subscriber or customer that the subscriber or customer has challenged the governmental entity's request; and

(B) has not initiated proceedings to challenge the request of the governmental entity.

(5) A governmental entity may seek to require the creation of a backup copy under subsection (a)(1) of this section if in its sole discretion such entity determines that there is reason to believe that notification under section 2703 of this title of the existence of the subpoena or court order may result in destruction of or tampering with evidence. This determination is not subject to challenge by the subscriber or customer or service provider.

(b) Customer Challenges. - (1) Within fourteen days after notice by the governmental entity to the subscriber or customer under subsection (a)(2) of this section, such subscriber or customer may file a motion to quash such subpoena or vacate such court order, with copies served upon the governmental entity and with written notice of such challenge to the service provider. A motion to vacate a court order shall be filed in the court which issued such order. A motion to quash a subpoena shall be filed in the appropriate United States district court or State court. Such motion or application shall contain an affidavit or sworn statement -

(A) stating that the applicant is a customer or subscriber to the service from which the contents of electronic communications maintained for him have been sought; and

(B) stating the applicant's reasons for believing that the records sought are not relevant to a legitimate law enforcement inquiry or that there has not been substantial compliance with the provisions of this chapter in some other respect.

(2) Service shall be made under this section upon a governmental entity by delivering or mailing by registered or certified mail a copy of the papers to the person, office, or department specified in the notice which the customer has received pursuant to this chapter. For the purposes of this section, the term "delivery" has the meaning given that term in the Federal Rules of Civil Procedure.

(3) If the court finds that the customer has complied with paragraphs (1) and (2) of this subsection, the court shall order the governmental entity to file a sworn response, which may be filed in camera if the governmental entity includes in its response the reasons which make in camera review appropriate. If the court is unable to determine the motion or application on the basis of the parties' initial allegations and response, the court may conduct such additional proceedings as it deems appropriate. All such proceedings shall be completed and the motion or application decided as soon as practicable after the filing of the governmental entity's response.

(4) If the court finds that the applicant is not the subscriber or customer for whom the communications sought by the governmental entity are maintained, or that there is a reason to believe that the law enforcement inquiry is legitimate and that the communications sought are relevant to that inquiry, it shall deny the motion or application and order such process enforced. If the court finds that the applicant is the subscriber or customer for whom the communications sought by the governmental entity are maintained, and that there is not a reason to believe that the communications sought are relevant to a legitimate law enforcement inquiry, or that there has not been substantial compliance with the provisions of this chapter, it shall order the process quashed.

(5) A court order denying a motion or application under

this section shall not be deemed a final order and no interlocutory appeal may be taken therefrom by the customer.

Title 18 Sec. 2705. Delayed notice

(a) Delay of Notification. - (1) A governmental entity acting under section 2703(b) of this title may -

(A) where a court order is sought, include in the application a request, which the court shall grant, for an order delaying the notification required under section 2703(b) of this title for a period not to exceed ninety days, if the court determines that there is reason to believe that notification of the existence of the court order may have an adverse result described in paragraph (2) of this subsection; or

(B) where an administrative subpoena authorized by a Federal or State statute or a Federal or State grand jury subpoena is obtained, delay the notification required under section 2703(b) of this title for a period not to exceed ninety days upon the execution of a written certification of a supervisory official that there is reason to believe that notification of the existence of the subpoena may have an adverse result described in paragraph (2) of this subsection.

(2) An adverse result for the purposes of paragraph (1) of this subsection is -

(A) endangering the life or physical safety of an individual;
(B) flight from prosecution;
(C) destruction of or tampering with evidence;
(D) intimidation of potential witnesses; or
(E) otherwise seriously jeopardizing an investigation or unduly delaying a trial.

(3) The governmental entity shall maintain a true copy of certification under paragraph (1)(B).

(4) Extensions of the delay of notification provided in section 2703 of up to ninety days each may be granted by the court upon application, or by certification by a governmental entity, but only in accordance with subsection (b) of this section.

(5) Upon expiration of the period of delay of notification under paragraph (1) or (4) of this subsection, the governmental entity shall serve upon, or deliver by registered or first-class mail to, the customer or subscriber a copy of the process or request together with notice that -
(A) states with reasonable specificity the nature of the law enforcement inquiry; and
(B) informs such customer or subscriber -
(i) that information maintained for such customer or subscriber by the service provider named in such process or request was supplied to or requested by that governmental authority and the date on which the supplying or request took place;
(ii) that notification of such customer or subscriber was delayed;
(iii) what governmental entity or court made the certification or determination pursuant to which that delay was made; and
(iv) which provision of this chapter allowed such delay.
(6) As used in this subsection, the term "supervisory official" means the investigative agent in charge or assistant investigative agent in charge or an equivalent of an investigating agency's headquarters or regional office, or the chief prosecuting attorney or the first assistant prosecuting attorney or an equivalent of a prosecuting attorney's headquarters or regional office.
(b) Preclusion of Notice to Subject of Governmental Access. - A governmental entity acting under section 2703, when it is not required to notify the subscriber or customer under section 2703(b)(1), or to the extent that it may delay such notice pursuant to subsection (a) of this section, may apply to a court for an order commanding a provider of electronic communications service or remote computing service to whom a warrant, subpoena, or court order is directed, for such period as the court deems appropriate, not to notify any other person of the existence of the warrant, subpoena, or court order. The court shall enter such an order if it deter-

Appendix III

mines that there is reason to believe that notification of the existence of the warrant, subpoena, or court order will result in -
    (1) endangering the life or physical safety of an individual;
    (2) flight from prosecution;
    (3) destruction of or tampering with evidence;
    (4) intimidation of potential witnesses; or
    (5) otherwise seriously jeopardizing an investigation or unduly delaying a trial.

Title 18 Sec. 2706. Cost reimbursement

(a) Payment. - Except as otherwise provided in subsection (c), a governmental entity obtaining the contents of communications, records, or other information under section 2702, 2703, or 2704 of this title shall pay to the person or entity assembling or providing such information a fee for reimbursement for such costs as are reasonably necessary and which have been directly incurred in searching for, assembling, reproducing, or otherwise providing such information. Such reimbursable costs shall include any costs due to necessary disruption of normal operations of any electronic communication service or remote computing service in which such information may be stored.

(b) Amount. - The amount of the fee provided by subsection (a) shall be as mutually agreed by the governmental entity and the person or entity providing the information, or, in the absence of agreement, shall be as determined by the court which issued the order for production of such information (or the court before which a criminal prosecution relating to such information would be brought, if no court order was issued for production of the information).

(c) Exception. - The requirement of subsection (a) of this section does not apply with respect to records or other information maintained by a communications common carrier that relate to telephone toll records and telephone listings obtained under section 2703 of this title. The court may, however, order a payment as described in subsection (a) if the court determines the information required is unusually voluminous in nature or otherwise caused an undue burden on the provider.

Title 18 Sec. 2707. Civil action

(a) Cause of Action. - Except as provided in section 2703(e), any provider of electronic communication service, subscriber, or other person aggrieved by any violation of this chapter in which the conduct constituting the violation is engaged in with a knowing or intentional state of mind may, in a civil action, recover from the person or entity which engaged in that violation such relief as may be appropriate.

(b) Relief. - In a civil action under this section, appropriate relief includes -

    (1) such preliminary and other equitable or declaratory relief as may be appropriate;

    (2) damages under subsection (c); and

    (3) a reasonable attorney's fee and other litigation costs reasonably incurred.

(c) Damages. - The court may assess as damages in a civil action under this section the sum of the actual damages suffered by the plaintiff and any profits made by the violator as a result of the violation, but in no case shall a person entitled to recover receive less than the sum of $1,000. If the violation is willful or intentional, the court may assess punitive damages. In the case of a successful action to enforce liability under this section, the court may assess the costs of the action, together with reasonable attorney fees determined by the court.

(d) Disciplinary Actions for Violations. - If a court determines that any agency or department of the United States has violated this chapter and the court finds that the circumstances surrounding the violation raise the question whether or not an officer or employee of the agency or department acted willfully or intentionally with respect to the violation, the agency or department concerned shall promptly initiate a proceeding to determine whether or not disciplinary action is warranted against the officer or employee.

(e) Defense. - A good faith reliance on -

Appendix III

(1) a court warrant or order, a grand jury subpoena, a legislative authorization, or a statutory authorization;
(2) a request of an investigative or law enforcement officer under section 2518(7) of this title; or
(3) a good faith determination that section 2511(3) of this title permitted the conduct complained of; is a complete defense to any civil or criminal action brought under this chapter or any other law.

(f) Limitation. - A civil action under this section may not be commenced later than two years after the date upon which the claimant first discovered or had a reasonable opportunity to discover the violation.

Title 18 Sec. 2708. Exclusivity of remedies

The remedies and sanctions described in this chapter are the only judicial remedies and sanctions for nonconstitutional violations of this chapter.

Title 18 Sec. 2709. Counterintelligence access to telephone toll and transactional records

(a) Duty to Provide. - A wire or electronic communication service provider shall comply with a request for subscriber information and toll billing records information, or electronic communication transactional records in its custody or possession made by the Director of the Federal Bureau of Investigation under subsection (b) of this section.

(b) Required Certification. - The Director of the Federal Bureau of Investigation, or his designee in a position not lower than Deputy Assistant Director, may -

(1) request the name, address, length of service, and local and long distance toll billing records of a person or entity if the Director (or his designee in a position not lower than Deputy Assistant Director) certifies in writing to the wire or electronic communication service provider to which the request is made that -

(A) the name, address, length of service, and toll billing records sought are relevant to an authorized foreign

counterintelligence investigation; and
(B) there are specific and articulable facts giving reason to believe that the person or entity to whom the information sought pertains is a foreign power or an agent of a foreign power as defined in section 101 of the Foreign Intelligence Surveillance Act of 1978 (50 U.S.C. 1801); and
(2) request the name, address, and length of service of a person or entity if the Director (or his designee in a position not lower than Deputy Assistant Director) certifies in writing to the wire or electronic communication service provider to which the request is made that -
(A) the information sought is relevant to an authorized foreign counterintelligence investigation; and
(B) there are specific and articulable facts giving reason to believe that communication facilities registered in the name of the person or entity have been used, through the services of such provider, in communication with -
(i) an individual who is engaging or has engaged in international terrorism as defined in section 101(c) of the Foreign Intelligence Surveillance Act or clandestine intelligence activities that involve or may involve a violation of the criminal statutes of the United States; or
(ii) a foreign power or an agent of a foreign power under circumstances giving reason to believe that the communication concerned international terrorism as defined in section 101(c) of the Foreign Intelligence Surveillance Act or clandestine intelligence activities that involve or may involve a violation of the criminal statutes of the United States.
(c) Prohibition of Certain Disclosure. - No wire or electronic communication service provider, or officer, employee, or agent thereof, shall disclose to any person that the Federal Bureau of Investigation has sought or obtained access to information or records under this section.
(d) Dissemination by Bureau. - The Federal Bureau of Investigation may disseminate information and records

obtained under this section only as provided in guidelines approved by the Attorney General for foreign intelligence collection and foreign counterintelligence investigations conducted by the Federal Bureau of Investigation, and, with respect to dissemination to an agency of the United States, only if such information is clearly relevant to the authorized responsibilities of such agency.

(e) Requirement That Certain Congressional Bodies Be Informed. - On a semiannual basis the Director of the Federal Bureau of Investigation shall fully inform the Permanent Select Committee on Intelligence of the House of Representatives and the Select Committee on Intelligence of the Senate, and the Committee on the Judiciary of the House of Representatives and the Committee on the Judiciary of the Senate, concerning all requests made under subsection (b) of this section.

Title 18 Sec. 2710. Wrongful disclosure of video tape rental or sale records

(a) Definitions. - For purposes of this section -

(1) the term "consumer" means any renter, purchaser, or subscriber of goods or services from a video tape service provider;

(2) the term "ordinary course of business" means only debt collection activities, order fulfillment, request processing, and the transfer of ownership;

(3) the term "personally identifiable information" includes information which identifies a person as having requested or obtained specific video materials or services from a video tape service provider; and

(4) the term "video tape service provider" means any person, engaged in the business, in or affecting interstate or foreign commerce, of rental, sale, or delivery of prerecorded video cassette tapes or similar audio visual materials, or any person or other entity to whom a disclosure is made under subparagraph (D) or (E) of subsection (b)(2), but only with respect to the information contained in the disclosure.

The Complete Guide to E-Security

(b) Video Tape Rental and Sale Records. - (1) A video tape service provider who knowingly discloses, to any person, personally identifiable information concerning any consumer of such provider shall be liable to the aggrieved person for the relief provided in subsection (d).

(2) A video tape service provider may disclose personally identifiable information concerning any consumer -

(A) to the consumer;

(B) to any person with the informed, written consent of the consumer given at the time the disclosure is sought;

(C) to a law enforcement agency pursuant to a warrant issued under the Federal Rules of Criminal Procedure, an equivalent State warrant, a grand jury subpoena, or a court order;

(D) to any person if the disclosure is solely of the names and addresses of consumers and if -

(i) the video tape service provider has provided the consumer with the opportunity, in a clear and con spicuous manner, to prohibit such disclosure; and

(ii) the disclosure does not identify the title, description, or subject matter of any video tapes or other audio visual material; however, the subject matter of such materials may be disclosed if the disclosure is for the exclusive use of marketing goods and services directly to the consumer;

(E) to any person if the disclosure is incident to the ordinary course of business of the video tape service provider; or

(F) pursuant to a court order, in a civil proceeding upon a showing of compelling need for the information that cannot be accommodated by any other means, if -

(i) the consumer is given reasonable notice, by the person seeking the disclosure, of the court proceeding relevant to the issuance of the court order; and

(ii) the consumer is afforded the opportunity to appear and contest the claim of the person seeking the disclosure. If an order is granted pursuant to subparagraph (c) or (F), the court shall impose appropri

Appendix III

ate safeguards against unauthorized disclosure.

(3) Court orders authorizing disclosure under subparagraph (c) shall issue only with prior notice to the consumer and only if the law enforcement agency shows that there is probable cause to believe that the records or other information sought are relevant to a legitimate law enforcement inquiry. In the case of a State government authority, such a court order shall not issue if prohibited by the law of such State. A court issuing an order pursuant to this section, on a motion made promptly by the video tape service provider, may quash or modify such order if the information or records requested are unreasonably voluminous in nature or if compliance with such order otherwise would cause an unreasonable burden on such provider.

(c) Civil Action. - (1) Any person aggrieved by any act of a person in violation of this section may bring a civil action in a United States district court.

(2) The court may award -

(A) actual damages but not less than liquidated damages in an amount of $2,500;

(B) punitive damages;

(C) reasonable attorneys' fees and other litigation costs reasonably incurred; and

(D) such other preliminary and equitable relief as the court determines to be appropriate.

(3) No action may be brought under this subsection unless such action is begun within 2 years from the date of the act complained of or the date of discovery.

(4) No liability shall result from lawful disclosure permitted by this section.

(d) Personally Identifiable Information. - Personally identifiable information obtained in any manner other than as provided in this section shall not be received in evidence in any trial, hearing, arbitration, or other proceeding in or before any court, grand jury, department, officer, agency, regulatory body, legislative committee, or other authority of the United States, a State, or a political subdivision of a State.

(e) Destruction of Old Records. - A person subject to this section shall destroy personally identifiable information as soon as practicable, but no later than one year from the date the information is no longer necessary for the purpose for which it was collected and there are no pending requests or orders for access to such information under subsection (b)(2) or (c)(2) or pursuant to a court order.
(f) Preemption. - The provisions of this section preempt only the provisions of State or local law that require disclosure prohibited by this section.

Title 18 Sec. 2711. Definitions for chapter

As used in this chapter -
(1) the terms defined in section 2510 of this title have, respectively, the definitions given such terms in that section; and
(2) the term "remote computing service" means the provision to the public of computer storage or processing services by means of an electronic communications system.

Appendix IV

CHILDREN'S ONLINE PRIVACY PROTECTION ACT
Title 15 United States Code Sec. 6501, et seq.

Definitions
In this chapter:
(1) Child
The term "child" means an individual under the age of 13.
(2) Operator
The term "operator" -
    (A) means any person who operates a website located on the Internet or an online service and who collects or maintains personal information from or about the users of or visitors to such website or online service, or on whose behalf such information is collected or maintained, where such website or online service is operated for commercial purposes, including any person offering products or services for sale through that website or online service, involving commerce -
        (i) among the several States or with 1 or more foreign nations;
        (ii) in any territory of the United States or in the District of Columbia, or between any such territory and -
            (I) another such territory; or
            (II) any State or foreign nation; or
        (iii) between the District of Columbia and any State, territory, or foreign nation; but
    (B) does not include any nonprofit entity that would otherwise be exempt from coverage under section 45 of this title.
(3) Commission
The term "Commission" means the Federal Trade Commission.
(4) Disclosure
The term "disclosure" means, with respect to personal information -
    (A) the release of personal information collected from a child in

The Complete Guide to E-Security

identifiable form by an operator for any purpose, except where such information is provided to a person other than the operator who provides support for the internal operations of the website and does not disclose or use that information for any other purpose; and
(B) making personal information collected from a child by a website or online service directed to children or with actual knowledge that such information was collected from a child, publicly available in identifiable form, by any means including by a public posting, through the Internet, or through -

    (i) a home page of a website;
    (ii) a pen pal service;
    (iii) an electronic mail service;
    (iv) a message board; or
    (v) a chat room.

(5) Federal agency
The term "Federal agency" means an agency, as that term is defined in section 551(1) of title 5.

(6) Internet
The term "Internet" means collectively the myriad of computer and telecommunications facilities, including equipment and operating software, which comprise the interconnected world-wide network of networks that employ the Transmission Control Protocol/Internet Protocol, or any predecessor or successor
protocols to such protocol, to communicate information of all kinds by wire or radio.

(7) Parent
The term "parent" includes a legal guardian.

(8) Personal information
The term "personal information" means individually identifiable information about an individual collected online, including -

    (A) a first and last name;
    (B) a home or other physical address including street name and name of a city or town;
    (C) an e-mail address;
    (D) a telephone number;
    (E) a Social Security number;
    (F) any other identifier that the Commission determines permits the physical or online contacting of a specific individual; or

Appendix IV

(G) information concerning the child or the parents of that child that the website collects online from the child and combines with an identifier described in this paragraph.

(9) Verifiable parental consent

The term "verifiable parental consent" means any reasonable effort (taking into consideration available technology), including a request for authorization for future collection, use, and disclosure described in the notice, to ensure that a parent of a child receives notice of the operator's personal information collection, use, and disclosure practices, and authorizes the collection, use, and disclosure, as applicable, of personal information and the subsequent use of that information before that information is collected from that child.

(10) Website or online service directed to children

(A) In general

The term "website or online service directed to children" means -

(i) a commercial website or online service that is targeted to children; or

(ii) that portion of a commercial website or online service that is targeted to children.

(B) Limitation

A commercial website or online service, or a portion of a commercial website or online service, shall not be deemed directed to children solely for referring or linking to a commercial website or online service directed to children by using information location tools, including a directory, index, reference, pointer, or hypertext link.

(11) Person

The term "person" means any individual, partnership, corporation, trust, estate, cooperative, association, or other entity.

(12) Online contact information

The term "online contact information" means an e-mail address or another substantially similar identifier that permits direct contact with a person online.

Sec. 6502. Regulation of unfair and deceptive acts and practices in connection with collection and use of personal information from and about children on the Internet

(a) Acts prohibited

(1) In general

It is unlawful for an operator of a website or online service directed to children, or any operator that has actual knowledge that it is collecting personal information from a child, to collect personal information from a child in a manner that violates the regulations prescribed under subsection (b) of this section.

(2) Disclosure to parent protected

Notwithstanding paragraph (1), neither an operator of such a website or online service nor the operator's agent shall be held to be liable under any Federal or State law for any disclosure made in good faith and following reasonable procedures in responding to a request for disclosure of personal information under subsection (b)(1)(B)(iii) of this section to the parent of a child.

(b) Regulations

(1) In general

Not later than 1 year after October 21, 1998, the Commission shall promulgate under section 553 of title 5 regulations that -

(A) require the operator of any website or online service directed to children that collects personal information from children or the operator of a website or online service that has actual knowledge that it is collecting personal information from a child -

(i) to provide notice on the website of what information is collected from children by the operator, how the operator uses such information, and the operator's disclosure practices for such information; and

(ii) to obtain verifiable parental consent for the collection, use, or disclosure of personal information from children;

(B) require the operator to provide, upon request of a parent under this subparagraph whose child has provided personal information to that website or online service, upon proper identification of that parent, to such parent -

(i) a description of the specific types of personal information collected from the child by that operator;

(ii) the opportunity at any time to refuse to permit the operator's further use or maintenance in retrievable form, or future online collection, of personal information from that child; and

(iii) notwithstanding any other provision of law, a means that is reasonable under the circumstances for the parent to

Appendix IV

obtain any personal information collected from that child;
(C) prohibit conditioning a child's participation in a game, the offering of a prize, or another activity on the child disclosing more personal information than is reasonably necessary to participate in such activity; and
(D) require the operator of such a website or online service to establish and maintain reasonable procedures to protect the confidentiality, security, and integrity of personal information collected from children.

(2) When consent not required

The regulations shall provide that verifiable parental consent under paragraph (1)(A)(ii) is not required in the case of -

(A) online contact information collected from a child that is used only to respond directly on a one-time basis to a specific request from the child and is not used to recontact the child and is not maintained in retrievable form by the operator;

(B) a request for the name or online contact information of a parent or child that is used for the sole purpose of obtaining parental consent or providing notice under this section and where such information is not maintained in retrievable form by the operator if parental consent is not obtained after a reasonable time;

(C) online contact information collected from a child that is used only to respond more than once directly to a specific request from the child and is not used to recontact the child beyond the scope of that request -

(i) if, before any additional response after the initial response to the child, the operator uses reasonable efforts to provide a parent notice of the online contact information collected from the child, the purposes for which it is to be used, and an opportunity for the parent to request that the operator make no further use of the information and that it not be maintained in retrievable form; or

(ii) without notice to the parent in such circumstances as the Commission may determine are appropriate, taking into consideration the benefits to the child of access to information and services, and risks to the security and privacy of the child, in regulations promulgated under this subsection;

(D) the name of the child and online contact information (to the

extent reasonably necessary to protect the safety of a child participant on the site) -
> (i) used only for the purpose of protecting such safety;
> (ii) not used to recontact the child or for any other purpose;
> (iii) not disclosed on the site,

if the operator uses reasonable efforts to provide a parent notice of the name and online contact information collected from the child, the purposes for which it is to be used, and an opportunity for the parent to request that the operator make no further use of the information and that it not be maintained in retrievable form; or

(E) the collection, use, or dissemination of such information by the operator of such a website or online service necessary -
> (i) to protect the security or integrity of its website;
> (ii) to take precautions against liability;
> (iii) to respond to judicial process; or
> (iv) to the extent permitted under other provisions of law,

to provide information to law enforcement agencies or for an investigation on a matter related to public safety.

(3) Termination of service

The regulations shall permit the operator of a website or an online service to terminate service provided to a child whose parent has refused, under the regulations prescribed under paragraph (1)(B)(ii), to permit the operator's further use or maintenance in retrievable form, or future online collection, of personal information from that child.

(c) Enforcement

Subject to sections 6503 and 6505 of this title, a violation of a regulation prescribed under subsection (a) of this section shall be treated as a violation of a rule defining an unfair or deceptive act or practice prescribed under section 57(a)(1)(B) of this title.

(d) Inconsistent State law

No State or local government may impose any liability for commercial activities or actions by operators in interstate or foreign commerce in connection with an activity or action described in this chapter that is inconsistent with the treatment of those activities or actions under this section.

Appendix IV

Sec. 6503. Safe harbors
(a) Guidelines
An operator may satisfy the requirements of regulations issued under section 6502(b) of this title by following a set of self-regulatory guidelines, issued by representatives of the marketing or online industries, or by other persons, approved under subsection (b) of this section.
(b) Incentives
    (1) Self-regulatory incentives
In prescribing regulations under section 6502 of this title, the Commission shall provide incentives for self-regulation by operators to implement the protections afforded children under the regulatory requirements described in subsection (b) of that section.
    (2) Deemed compliance
    Such incentives shall include provisions for ensuring that a person will be deemed to be in compliance with the requirements of the regulations under section 6502 of this title if that person complies with guidelines that, after notice and comment, are approved by the Commission upon making a determination that the guidelines meet the requirements of the regulations issued under section 6502 of this title.
    (3) Expedited response to requests
    The Commission shall act upon requests for safe harbor treatment within 180 days of the filing of the request, and shall set forth in writing its conclusions with regard to such requests.
(c) Appeals
Final action by the Commission on a request for approval of guidelines, or the failure to act within 180 days on a request for approval of guidelines, submitted under subsection (b) of this section may be appealed to a district court of the United States of appropriate jurisdiction as provided for in section 706 of title 5.

Bibliography

Bacard, André. *The Computer Privacy Handbook.* Berkeley, California: Peachpit Press, 1995.

Beeson, Ann. *Privacy in Cyberspace: Is Your E-mail Safe from the Boss, the SysOp, the Hackers, and the Cops?* American Civil Liberties Union, 1996. **(http://www.aclu.org/issues/cyber/priv/privpap.html)**

Clark, Franklin, and Ken Diliberto. *Investigating Computer Crime.* Boca Raton, Florida: CRC Press, 1996.

Davis, Peter T., and Barry D. Lewis. *Computer Security for Dummies.* Foster City, California: IDG Books, 1996.

Fiery, Dennis (Knightmare). *Secrets of a Super Hacker.* Port Townsend, Washington: Loompanics Unlimited, 1994.

Nickels, Hamilton. *Codemaster: Secrets of Making and Breaking Codes.* Boulder, Colorado: Paladin Press, 1990.

Quarantiello, Laura E. *Cyber Crime: How to Protect Yourself from Computer Criminals*. Lake Geneva, Wisconsin: Tiare Publications, 1997.

Schneier, Bruce. *E-mail Security: How to Keep Your Electronic Messages Private*, New York, New York: John Wiley & Sons, Inc., 1995.

Schwartau, Winn. *Information Warfare*. New York: Thunder's Mouth Press, 1994.

Stallings, William, Ph.D. *Network and Internetwork Security Principles and Practice*. Upper Saddle River, New Jersey: Prentice-Hall, Inc., 1995.

Weise, Elizabeth. "'Self-destruct' E-mail Offers Virtual Privacy," *USA Today*, 23 November 1999, , PM edition

Wrixon, Fred R. *Codes, Ciphers, and Secret Languages*. New York: Bonanza Books, 1989.

About the Author

Michael Chesbro is a senior counterintelligence agent with the U.S. Department of Defense. He holds degrees in security management and in jurisprudence and is a graduate of the Federal Law Enforcement Training Center. He is professionally certified as a protection officer and as a security supervisor by the International Foundation for Protection Officers. He is a board-certified forensic examiner and fellow of the American College of Forensic Examiners, as well as a diplomate of the American Board of Forensic Examiners and the American Board of Law Enforcement Experts.